DARK AND STORMY RIDES AGAIN

Scott Rice is a professor at San Jose State University and the creator of the Bulwer-Lytton Fiction Contest. Born in Lewiston, Idaho, and raised in Spokane, Washington, he received his B.A. from Gonzga University and his M.A. and Ph.D. from the University of Arizona. Scott Rice is married and the father of three children: Jeremy, Matthew, and Elizabeth. He is also the compiler if *It Was a Dark and Stormy Night, Son of "It Was a Dark and Stormy Night," Bride of Dark and Stormy*, and *It Was a Dark & Stormy Night: The Final Conflict* (all available from Penguin).

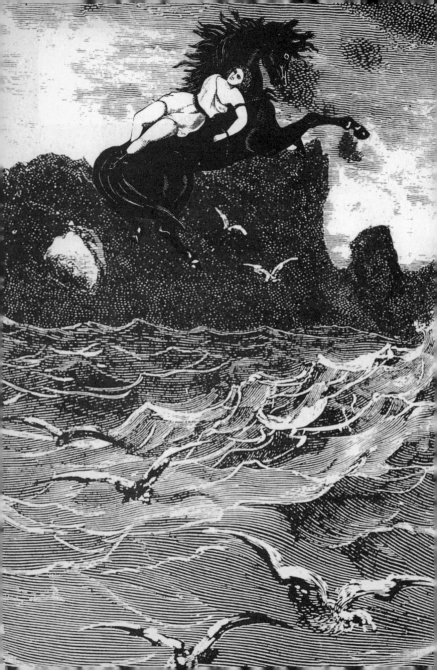

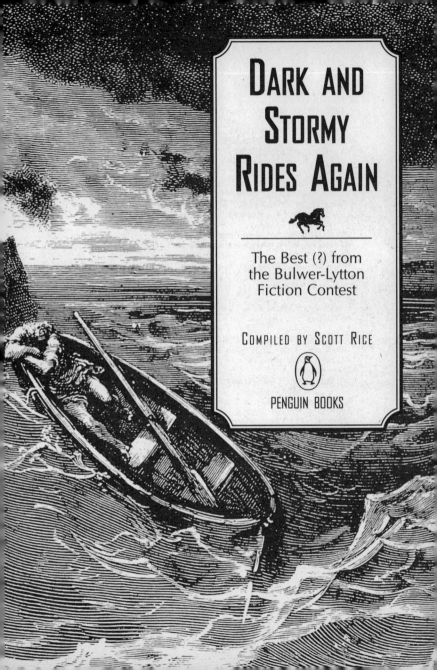

Dark and Stormy Rides Again

The Best (?) from
the Bulwer-Lytton
Fiction Contest

Compiled by Scott Rice

Penguin Books

PENGUIN BOOKS
Published by the Penguin Group
Penguin Books USA Inc., 375 Hudson Street,
New York, New York 10014, U.S.A.
Penguin Books Ltd, 27 Wrights Lane,
London W8 5TZ, England
Penguin Books Australia Ltd, Ringwood,
Victoria, Australia
Penguin Books Canada Ltd, 10 Alcorn Avenue,
Toronto, Ontario, Canada M4V 3B2
Penguin Books (N.Z.) Ltd, 182–190 Wairau Road,
Auckland 10, New Zealand

Penguin Books Ltd, Registered Offices:
Harmondsworth, Middlesex, England

First published in Penguin Books 1996

10 9 8 7 6 5 4 3 2 1

Copyright © Scott Rice, 1996
All rights reserved

LIBRARY OF CONGRESS CATALOGING IN PUBLICATION DATA
Dark and stormy rides again: the best (?) from the Bulwer-Lytton
    Contest/compiled by Scott Rice.
        p.   cm.
    ISBN 0 14 02.5490 0 (pbk.)
    1. Authorship—Humor.   2. Style, Literary—Humor.   3. Fiction—
Technique—Humor.   4. English language—Style—Humor.   I. Rice,
Scott.   II. Bulwer-Lytton Contest.
PN6231.A77D37   1996
818´.5408—dc20   95–50537

Printed in the United States of America
Set in Caslon 540
Designed by Virginia Norey

Except in the United States of America, this book is
sold subject to the condition that it shall not, by way of
trade or otherwise, be lent, re-sold, hired out, or otherwise
circulated without the publisher's prior consent in any form
of binding or cover other than that in which it is published
and without a similar condition including this condition
being imposed on the subsequent purchaser.

Contents

INTRODUCTION

The Bulwer-Lytton Fiction Contest is an annual international competition that invites entrants to compose bad opening sentences to imaginary novels. The contest takes its name from the esteemed Victorian novelist Edward George Bulwer-Lytton (1803–73), perhaps best known for *The Last Days of Pompeii*, but also responsible for coining such expressions as "the great unwashed" and "the pen is mightier than the sword" (from his play, *Richelieu*). Bulwer was that rare genius who could extrude instant clichés—expressions immediately stale. A Shakespeare, a Milton, or a Wordsworth must wait at least a century or two before some particular phraseology suffers the wear of over-familiarity. Not so for Bulwer. Readers immediately recognized the timeworn quality of "It was a dark and stormy night" (from *Paul Clifford*, 1830), as they did a paragraph later, where a character is seen "wending his solitary way." Bulwer was a wordsmith sans pareil—you might even say, without equal.

The contest was first held at San Jose State University in 1982 and, after an auspicious inaugural year (three entries), it went public. The rest is history, sort of. Each year thousands of entrants vie for the honor (or at least the notoriety) of being another Bulwer. The contest has become such a cultural fixture, like cable spots for Richard Simmons' exercise videos, that some people like to think that the Bulwer-Lytton Fiction Contest has assumed a place alongside the Nobel and Pulitzer prizes for literature. (Of course, some of these same people like to think that butter and whipped cream are good for their middle-aged arteries.) Granted, a slightly larger number consider it the literary equivalent of making loud noises with one's armpits, but—on this most pressing of subjects—the discerning reader must be the final judge. Which, of course, leaves you out.

1992 Winner

As the newest Lady Turnpot descended into the kitchen wrapped only in her celery-green dressing gown, her creamy bosom rising and falling like a temperamental soufflé, her tart mouth pursed in distaste, the sous-chef whispered to the scullery boy, "I don't know what to make of her."

—*Laurel Fortuner*
Montendre, France

1993 Winner

She really wasn't my type, a hard-looking but untalented reporter for the local cat-box liner, but the first second that that third-rate representative of the fourth estate cracked open a new fifth of old Scotch, my sixth sense said seventh heaven was as close as an eighth note from Beethoven's Ninth Symphony, so, nervous as a tenth grader drowning in eleventh-hour cramming for a physics exam, I swept her into my longing arms, and, humming the "The Twelfth of Never," I got lucky on Friday the thirteenth.

—Wm. W. "Buddy" Ocheltree
Port Townsend, Washington

1994 Winner

As the fading light of a dying day filtered through the window blinds, Roger stood over his victim with a smoking .45, surprised at the serenity that filled him after pumping six slugs into the bloodless tyrant that mocked him day after day, and then he shuffled out of the office with one last look back at the shattered computer terminal lying there like a silicon armadillo left to rot on the information superhighway.

—Larry Brill
Austin, Texas

1995 Winner

Paul Revere had just discovered that someone in Boston was a spy for the British, and when he saw the young woman believed to be the spy's girlfriend in an Italian restaurant he said to the waiter, "Hold the spumoni—I'm going to follow the chick an' catch a Tory."

—John L. Ashman
Houston, Texas

PURPLE PROSE

With a curvaceous figure that Venus would have envied, a tanned unblemished oval face framed with lustrous thick brown hair, deep azure-blue eyes fringed with long black lashes, perfect teeth that vied for competition, and a small straight nose, Marilee had a beauty that defied description.
—*Alice A. Hall*
Fort Wayne, Indiana

The long narrow road stretched out before her like a string of cheese from a hot pepperoni pizza (you know, the kind that is just out of the oven and much too hot to eat but you bite into it anyway and it burns you and leaves little bits of seared flesh dangling from the roof of your mouth that you tongue gingerly for the next week) in the early morning light.
—*Jim Sanderson*
Portland, Oregon

The sun crept up into the crack of dawn like cheap underwear.
—*Cindy Baran*
New York, New York

The moon hung full and swollen like a pimple on the adolescent face of night.
—*Marc Paul Kohler*
Philadelphia, Pennsylvania

The full moon jutted out like a malevolent speed bump on the blacktop of night.
—*Donny Philicione*
Belleville, New Jersey

To Felicity, Lyle was more, much more, than the other men she had known, for beyond that overall-and-axlegrease exterior, he was a true mechanic of romance, able to pound the dents out of the fenders of her soul, to balance the tires of her psyche, to gap the spark plugs of her ardor, and to spin her heart like a wing-nut on the bolt of his love.
—*Vance Atkins*
Seattle, Washington

In the same way a chicken embryo grows inside of its small, round, white, hard but fragile sphere, the thought began to take form inside Leroy's head, small at first like a mutant pygmy hummingbird but eventually expanding to near ostrich proportions, until finally it launched into majestic flight, smacking lobes of his brain the way a sparrow repeatedly tries to fly through a closed window (consequently causing the left side of Leroy's upper lip to twitch slightly), until the thought, like that brave little sparrow, tried one time too many to get through and broke its neck before it could transform itself into words and pass through Leroy's cracked, flaking, sunburnt lips, so it just lay there hacking up blood until, just like the dodo bird, it fizzled into extinction.
—*Jennifer S. Anderson*
San Jose, California

"Best not pester Mr. Buster's sister Hester, blast her, lest her blisters fester," rasped our flustered pastor.
—*Gwen Fuller*
Menlo Park, California

I burst out of bed like a gas bubble and limped determinedly to the gazebo where, overhead, jet aeroplanes, like modern metal slugs, trailed their vapor slime across the sidewalks of the sky, and thought then that this Thursday would be like any other.   —*H. Gordon Havens*
Independence, Missouri

Rose leafed through *Getting to the Root of Your Problems Before Going to Seed* by Sap Ling of the Pine Nut Society when she recalled Bud, branching one arm around her pear-shaped, draped-in-mock-orange trunk, needling her by passing to Fern's palm a wisteria bouquet thus sprouting in her life the dilemma posed in the Blight-of-the-Month book—yew either "nip the Bud," "plum give up," or accept "tree's 'de vine."   —*Ann Fowler*
Herington, Kansas

Oh, I can remember how grim and forlorn it was, that miserable place where a vomit-colored sky kissed the ocean whose errant children, the massive silver waves, crashed like suicidal whales against the bleakness, the dismal stone cliffs of Primal Scream Point, squashing their frothy white heads on the rocks and sliding like deflated sex dolls into the sands below where they vanished silently like a group of aged, incoherent hookers simply worn to a frazzle.   —*Jene Moseley*
Silver City, New Mexico

It was July, and hotter than Hades in Jalisco, a jillion miles from LaJolla where he was to meet Julio, Jesus, and Jack, and his stomach had already jettisoned his lunch of jalapeños and Jujubes, giving Javior one more reason to hate juntas.   —*Shirley Stedem Young*
Shelter Cove, California

Alexis, at the nexus of her teenaged life, felt in her solar plexus that she had to have her daddy's Lexus when her family moved to Texas.

—*Brien Dolan*
Campbell River, British Columbia

There is a balm in Gilead, not a liniment, nor an ointment of sorts, just a balm; not so much a salve as an emollient; unguent doesn't fully define the lubricative nature of this balm, grease seems even too pejorative and creosote too oafish; it's not wax, fat, tallow, or lard; it's a lotion, a cerate, a cream, a demulcent, an unction; yet, there it is in Gilead.

—*David Headrick*
Riverside, California

As my prepubescent ears pensively perceived the pitter-patter of precipitation pounding the pristine purple roof of my parents' ponderous Pontiac, the whoosh-whooshing of windshield wipers wove an ever-widening awareness which would forever fan the flames of future forays into flights of fantasy; and as the car lost contact with the concrete and careened against the containment walls of the causeway, causing the nausea and amnesia that still gnaws at my craw, it was then I knew—I would be a writer.

—*Ray St. Louis*
Alachua, Florida

Alexandra's mind hovered between sleepiness and wakefulness until the alarm clock, that harbinger of temporal existence, blared like Gabriel's trumpet in her ears, sounding like the labor cries of Mother Time giving birth to a new day.

—*Suzanne J. Morgan*
Rochester, New York

As Sonia entered the ballroom, her despair cascaded to the parquet like ionized salts in a faulty centrifuge, to steal from Tolstoy.
—*James Thielman*
Sioux Falls, South Dakota

Gaia is a carnivore consuming our tree-coffined corpses in her great digestive tract like so many earth-powdered truffles; she exhales our smoking cremated remains like so many acrid cheroots; our watery decomposing flesh is but a salty rind to be swizzled in her deep despairing drink, thought Maddy, glumly, as she gazed at the bleak Vancouver sky.
—*S. Krickhan*
Vancouver, British Columbia

"Well, punk, was it two shots or three? I'm afraid that in all this excitement I lost count," hissed the vengeful espresso attendant, squinting into the overcast Seattle glare from behind a travel mug of steaming latte, "You have to ask yourself, 'Do I feel wired today?' Well, do you?"
—*Vance Atkins*
Seattle, Washington

Angel was a floozie, Hanson knew that, but in her bright red, latex mini-dress (sold as a top) she was a stunner, and her image dazzled the pixels of his brain like a midnight shelling of Sarajevo, or perhaps they just glowed in vivid, stunning reproduction, like high-definition TV presenting the Rose Parade, as he stared, mesmerized, thinking her fluid lines were like hot lava flowing sensuously down the sloping hills and crevices of a pouting volcano, topped by a smoldering cloud of "big" black hair, or maybe like a red candle, melting slowly in the hot sun, twisting sensuously and forming into soft, suggestive shapes, aided, perhaps, by an imaginative finger, or as if her naked torso had been dipped in that red plastic stuff used to put a grip on the cheap pliers you keep in your glove compartment; but, even after prolonged reflection, all he could say for certain was that she was *not* like the cheap dipped pliers in his glove compartment.

—*David Kenway*
Douglas, Alaska

By the time he got back from Tulsa, it was clear that the nagging little worm of doubt had eaten a substantial hole in the pure white daikon of Mabel's affections.

—*Sarah Sherwood*
Eugene, Oregon

VILE
PUNS

Guido Marishino looked at his Thompson submachine gun, with its gentle spiral of smoke climbing from the once-flaming muzzle, then looked at the crumpled, bullet-ridden body of the street performer with his blood-spattered make-up, and realized with sadness that, no matter how much money they had paid him to do it, a mime was a terrible thing to waste.
—*Brian J. Bargender, Inc.*
Wausau, Wisconsin

Ralph, Fred, Howard, and I often race each other across the lake in our leaky old rowboats, and it's not uncommon for us to take on a lot of water, but it never ceases to amaze us to see the level to which Howard's stern will sink.
—*Wm. W. "Buddy" Ocheltree*
Port Townsend, Washington

There is a legend among the Paris railroad repairmen that during the 1800s, if a section of track was found to be too unstable for safety, all you had to do was yell out, "Too loose, lay track!" and a small dwarf would show up and paint your picture.
—*Richard W. O'Bryan*
Perrysburg, Ohio

After working the crowd, the autograph hound lacked only the signature of the vice president's wife, so when he spotted her at the far edge of the field, he called to his friend, "Come on, it's a long way to Tipper, Harry!"

—*Barbara Stegman*
Del Mar, California

The ex-weightlifter/director started the rehearsals by telling us, "Okay, we gonna be baroque composers in dis one; you be Telleman, you be Vivaldi, und I'll be Bach."

—*Richard Patching*
Calgary, Alberta

"Drip, drip, drip, drip," thought Jane as she scanned her mental Roladex for an escort to the annual Plumber's Ball.

—*Michael David Edwards*
Everett, Washington

After savaging the pansies, the gastropod turned his attention to the roses: "So many beauties," he sighed, "so little slime."

—*Mary Anthony*
Grand Rapids, Michigan

Held at bay, feeling like a skewered onion under the raw stare of those two, cold, potato eyes, she wanted to flee the stranger's presence, but found herself instead confessing to the horror that seethed like an unwelcome bacon rind, simmering in the rich milky stockpot of her memories, making a chowder of her life: the silence of the clams.

—*Lin Dane*
Little River, California

There was considerable consternation among the cats in the Coliseum when it was learned that the tigers were taking the lions' share of the prophets.
—*Gary S. Dunbar*
Cooperstown, New York

Who would have thought that he would woo her, he a Christian and she a devout Muslim, all summer long without avail.

—*Bill Mott-Smith*
Oakland, California

At the turn of one of the centuries, a visiting interior decorator admiring the rainbow-like koi in the moat of the emperor's palace in Tokyo was told that the koi were in reality carp, and when leaning closer to better watch the fascinating fish, his wallet fell out of his pocket into the moat where a carp quickly grasped it in his mouth, and the interior decorator, gratified that it was caught by a fish and not allowed to sink to the bottom of the deep moat, grabbed for the fish to retrieve his wallet, whereupon the carp surprisingly passed it to one of his fellows, at which the decorator marveled but grabbed for the other fish, only to have that one, too, pass the wallet to another fish, when suddenly he realized that he had discovered carp-to-carp walleting.

—*William R. Appel*
Hilmar, California

The medieval barber continued to bleed the ailing Mordrid, chanting unintelligibly now and then, knowing that at any moment his leech might exceed his clasp.

—*Rix Quinn*
Fort Worth, Texas

Michelle Thibideaux, having just finished her final-round performance in the International Speed Signing Competition sponsored by the American Calligraphic Society—Signature Division, was anxiously awaiting the final entry (Sister Grizelda of the Holy Order of the Apotheosis and Car Wash), when her coach approached her and said worriedly, "You were fast, kid, but wait 'til the nun signs, Shelly."

—*Brian Taylor*
Novi, Michigan

Loretta had been working as the tattoo artist's assistant for only two weeks and already he had designs on her.

—*Hugh B. King*
Fremont, California

"I hate being saddled with this job," griped Perry Mutual, the mane man, "and, hay, I refuse to curry favor or go to great lengths just to jockey for position, and besides . . ." he bridled, "I'll bet that horse's behind isn't the stable influence he appears to be, not a bit; and if he thinks he can give me the brush, I'll teach him to stay away from my turf; and he's just grandstanding anyway, or at least it's a stall, because you know he loves to stirrup trouble and go against the grain, and he's definitely on the wrong track; you can make book on that."

—*Kathy Gire*
Loomis, California

"I hate goat's cheese!" she called out, her shrill voice startling the other diners, but it was too late, for even while the sound of her words was still echoing through the room the waiter placed the Greek salad before her and it was clear to all that it was a *fait accompli*.

—*Christopher Long*
Austin, Texas

The desert car lot's biggest problem was removing sand from their autos, so much, in fact, that a large sand removal hose (dubbed "A") and a smaller hose ("B") were both available for the task and confused the novice washer-boy who asked his manager if sand hose "B" was the proper

choice for this day's work and was told, no, that after the previous night's heavy wind, today's condition constituted a sand hose "A" state.
—*Richard Heine*
Whittier, California

Incensed when he heard the two monks who lived in a cottage at the end of town had been rude to the mayor when he confronted them about inadvertently raising among their usual vegetables a man-eating plant that had eaten a village child; Hugh, the village idiot and strong man, kicked their door open, grabbed the two monks by their necks, and told them that, if they ever raised another man-eating plant, he would personally break their heads; and they obeyed, thus proving the old adage: "Hugh, and only Hugh, can prevent florist friars."
—*Ron Horne*
Kentfield, Washington

Ever the soldier and seldom the diplomat, John Smith worried about the consequences of having taken a swing at Chief Powhatan, and nervously inquired of his lieutenant, "Will that poke, uh, haunt us?"
—*Jeremy Matthews*
Coopers Droop, Tennessee

Rosemary clove to her own thoughts and hurt feelings as she watched her butler, Herb, gingerly cross the room and then leave after she peppered the old salt with accusations about Harry Gano the gardener, and decided that she would make up with her sweet Basil while ruing the time she had wasted on the unsavory sin-a-minute Terry, gone now with her heart and her heirloom spice rack.
—*Richard Patching*
Calgary, Alberta

MIKE HARDWARE, P.I.

Mike Hardware was the kind of private eye who didn't know the meaning of the word "fear," a man who could laugh in the face of danger and spit in the eye of death—in short, a moron with suicidal tendencies.

—*Eddie Lawhorn*
Huntsville, Alabama

Two things made the case interesting, greed and sex; it was about greedy sex and sexy greed, it was about sex for money, piles of money, about money for sex, piles of sex, and ultimately about sex in piles of money, but only one thing made me take the case—greed, well, actually two things: greed and sex. —*Joe Becker*
Gig Harbor, Washington

"Yes, I am Sherlock Holmes, and you must be my new assistant; your name is Watson, you like to eat Ho-Ho's, you hail from America, you have a drinking problem, you voted for Gerald Ford, your favorite film is *Shanghai Surprise*, you fantasize about Madonna because you've never had a woman in real life, and unless I miss my guess, you listen to Barry Manilow," said Sherlock Holmes, and I knew right away I'd hate working for him.

—*Bill Bystricky*
Sunnyvale, California

As I drove down from L.A. to look into that case involving a midget from Caracas who blew away Sonny "the Boner" DiBono in the parking lot of the Potted Palms Trailer Park, Palm Springs looked like one of those silly drinks with celery and little bitty umbrellas sticking outta them.
—*Leslie Applegarth Farrer*
Berkeley, California

Benedict, the boiling sun poaching his brain already scrambled by a crack to the back of the head, and blood congealing on his hair like ketchup on powdered eggs, had been on the case only three minutes: a grade-A hard-boiled detective.
—*Juanita Cannon*
Overland Park, Kansas

They say it's a dog-eat-dog world, and this morning the fur was really flying at the old rat race—secretaries had their claws out, accountants circled the bottom line like hawks, the boss bulled his way through the meeting like a rogue elephant with a tusk ache, and, when they weren't wolfing down doughnuts, the salesmen parroted back his clichés like birds of a feather flocking together—but none of it had me buffaloed because I'd written my letter of resignation and I was in hog heaven, as optimistic as a Chihuahua in love with a Saint Bernard, leaving the herd behind to take a position as head of the pack at Hairball and Associates.
—*Carolyn J. Rose*
Portland, Oregon

"You can run," shouted Scotland Yard's Inspector Boothroyd in triumph as he clutched the last remaining bottle of noxious potion and watched Dr. Jekyll leap to

freedom through the shattered laboratory window, "but you can't Hyde."
                                                    —*Robert L. Bryant Jr.*
                                                    Columbia, South Carolina

I deduced that Nadia McMurphy's prostrate body had been dead at least four hours: the underside of her unattractive, bikini-clad form—her belly, in this case—was discolored with a purplish stain under the skin caused by the settling of her non-circulating blood surrendering to the pull of gravity; rigor mortis had begun in the small muscles of her fingers and slack, staring face; her arms and legs were blue and the temperature of her body was 92.4 degrees Fahrenheit, down 6.2 degrees from normal 98.6 . . . yes, there are over a thousand homicides in the Detroit metropolitan area every year, and I know about all of 'em; but it's not my job, I just like talking about dead people.   —*Melissa Anne Eggertsen*
                                                    Rochester Hills, Michigan

His labored breathing resembled that of a dentist's spit sucker, and small wonder, since that is what a .44 slug fired at point blank range into the chest of an asthmatic is wont to do.   —*Mary Kerr*
                                                    San Mateo, California

as i sit here moments before i swing from the gallows i wonder how inspector thompson-baker concluded by the note which read "you, sir arthur mitchell, will be in the london morgue before friday" that i, e. e. cummings, an american poet visiting the united kingdom, had indeed committed the market street murder on st. patrick's day.   —*Ernie Santilli*
                                                    Drexel Hill, Pennsylvania

Like the ever-changing-color scales of an opalescent rain forest chameleon, like the bilious neon and fluorescent lights in the Bowery at New Year's, like a low-hanging traffic signal struck by lightning, like Fourth of July fireworks seen through a sweaty cheerleader's T-shirt from the backseat of a 1964 Chevy convertible during a hailstorm in Dubuque, like flushing a cherry bomb down the john in the boys' locker room during the P.E. final, abruptly, a color-burst of sulfur flowers, Chinese pinwheels, exotic strippers' tassels, sequined G-strings and three cans of iridescent, overripe SPAM exploded behind Johnny Flamingo's steely blue eyes inside his immaculately-coiffed blond skull, and he knew he'd been coldcocked again.

—*Terrence O. Carroll*
San Jose, California

The door was locked from the outside, the windows were closed and had heavy shutters bolted from the outside, and although we searched carefully we could not find any access to the room from the floor, ceiling, walls, or fireplace, so only one thing kept this from being a perfect locked-door mystery—the corpse was in the hall.

—*Richard W. O'Bryan*
Perrysburg, Ohio

It had been eight or nine years since Lieutenant Ed "Ted" Blanderman had so much as thought about women; even the musky, manly, testosterone-laced aroma of his armpit shoulder holster now failed to remind him of her, so he found it odd and frightening that something so innocuous, so trivial, so commonplace as penetrating the dark leathern recess of his hip holster with the hard blue-steel nose of his .44 would, without warning, bring the image of

the ravishing necrophiliac Heather thrusting past his panting and moaning id into the steamy bullpen of his conscious mind.
—Mary A. Harrison
Marietta, Georgia

Inspector McMurkee pulled up the collar of his trench coat, for the fog along the Thames was thick and the Inspector could see only ten feet in front of him, which McMurkee figured was just about right since he was tailing the Heidelberg Quintet.
—John L. Ashman
Houston, Texas

Sure, I knew that worshiping golden calves went against every rule in the book, but when Victoria Brennaman strolled hers (toned and tanned as they were) into my place of business ("Jack Jarvis, Private Investigations—Indiscretions Handled With Discretion" it says on the shingle), I decided to shelve that book on my dusty windowsill and concentrated on getting those gorgeous gams onto my full-size Posturpedic altar, pronto.
—Chris Austin
Crawfordsville, Indiana

After P.J. heard the APB on the CB in his RV, he switched on the A/C and sped through NYC with WPLJ blaring on the FM dial—someone was bound to be DOA if he didn't get to the mall ASAP, for only he knew the suspect's true M.O., which, FYI, was pretty twisted, involving S and M with CVS employees using spare NASA parts and K-Y Jelly.
—Frank M. Carrano
Branford, Connecticut

My first sight of her was from across the floor, but even at that distance, the alarms went off, not the loud sirens of a fire truck on its way to a four-alarm fire, no, this was more like the shrill sound that only dogs and wild animals, steeped in primordial instincts, can hear, and which cries out in a universal language, "Do not stop at 'Go,' turn and run, as fast as your short little varicose-vein-infested legs can take you—this chick is trouble!"

—*Michele M. Ferrier*
San Francisco, California

At the sight of his superior's decapitated body, gorge rose in Detective Max Angst's throat, stopped for a smoke and read last night's meaty graffiti on his back teeth, then took the A train to his shiny black shoes.

—*Joseph E. Murphy*
Fairbanks, Alaska

When the dame with hair the color of an L.A. smog-alert sunset and pouting flame-red lips waltzed through the door of Frank's Dingy Diner, creating her own microclimate with the sinus-stinging scent of cheap perfume, and with the big dark eyes of a Walter Keane painting, her hips swinging in an invitation as old as time, she made my mouth feel like a half-ton bale of stale cotton and my weakened composure unraveled like the plot of a bad detective story as the coffee cup shook in my hands and my grandfather's favorite phrase echoed through my brain—"It must be cream, 'cause milk don't shimmy like that."

—*Toni Mayer*
El Cerrito, California

It was a tough city, cold, greasy, and crumbling around the edges like a meatloaf left too long in the refrigerator, the kind of city where a mug would sell his mother without a second thought, except she was probably already working a street corner somewhere and he would have to buy her first.
—D. F. Farmwald
South Bend, Indiana

The rain fell, the lightning struck, the thunder clapped, the clock chimed, the phone rang, the lights failed, the maid screamed, the stairs creaked, the dog barked, the shadow lunged, the gun fired, the body slumped, the gardener ran, the doorbell rang, the detective appeared, the suspects assembled, the majority lied, the butler confessed, the storm ended, the detective left.
—Peter A. Samish
Lake View Terrace, California

Nick "Buzzard" Brawley had a rep for being a hard guy, but his flat, black eyes were beginning to show an oil slick of unease as Harry Maxford, the LAPD's top interrogator, relentlessly hammered at him, "Y-y-you s-s-say, you say, y-y-you w-w-were at-at-at M-M-Maury's in G-G-Gardena when the, when the j-j-job w-w-went d-d-down?—Buh-buh-bullshit, N-N-Nick, I don't, I don't b-b-buy that f-f-for a m-m-minute, n-n-not when Lam-Lam-LeMar L-L-Lincoln c-c-claims he was, was s-s-slippin' you a d-d-dime b-bag at N-N-Ninth and-and-and F-F-Figueroa n-n-not ten, not ten, not ten m-m-minutes earlier."
—Cynthia Conyers
Warner Springs, California

"No, it's definitely pus," cocksure twenty-five-year veteran police detective Stewart McGill proclaimed after
licking the sample of evidence from his index finger
and tasting it carefully, destroying cadet Stevens' vanilla-
custard theory and feeling damn proud that he could still
teach the "new kids" a thing or two.

—*Michael David Edwards*
Everett, Washington

Popular British biographer Lady Elspeth Spenserhill
announced today that, upon advice of her counsel, T. Ar-
buthnot Brewster, K.B.E., she had engaged renowned
private investigator Padric O'Hallorin to locate research
material for her latest book, the unpublished letters and
photographs pertaining to the late Madame Lidja "Tardi"
Petronovskaya's scandalous 1920s liaison with the German
steel magnate Baron Gerhaupt von Reichsfall-Pasoune,
reported missing by Lady Spenserhill's secretary, Elder-
ton MacKenzie, recovering from the loss of two toes a
fortnight earlier in a mysterious boating mishap near
Walton-on-Thames still under investigation by Scotland
Yard.

—*Dolores Dueber Stevens*
Palo Alto, California

"I shall," I said, stooping to pick up my trusty revolver
and a sack of Dr. Pepper cans as a half-chewed Flintstones
vitamin tablet flew out of my mouth and onto the front
steps of the aluminum recycling facility where "Legs"
O'Reilly supposedly worked, "return."

—*Jeff Richards*
West Valley City, Utah

Coroner Jones carefully examined the battered corpse, checking for any tiny clue that might help identify the deranged serial killer, and, finding none, cheerfully pushed the body over the cliff and drove home to set up his alibi.

—Eddie Lawhorn
Huntsville, Alabama

LYTTONY
I

FROM *It Was a Dark and Stormy Night* (1984)

The sun oozed over the horizon, shoved aside darkness, crept along the greensward, and, with sickly fingers, pushed through the castle window, revealing the pillaged princess, hand at throat, crown asunder, gaping in frenzied horror at the sated, sodden amphibian lying beside her, disbelieving the magnitude of the toad's deception, screaming madly, "You lied!"
—*Barbara Kroll*
Kennett Square, Pennsylvania

It was only a matter of time before the alarm clock rang.
—*Graham Reader*
Calgary, Alberta

"It *really* is not as easy as it *looks!*" said Andrecau Ptolomi to his friend Albert Einstein, as he twisted the eucalyptus twig to form an electrical outlet.
—*Elias-Axel Petterrson*
Albuquerque, New Mexico

The Supremes, responding penitently to the judgment of their critics, changed their group's name to the Earnest, Moderately-Talented Young Women Who Sing for a Living.
—*Rev. William F. Charles*
Cassopolis, Michigan

Luther Framwell had been dumpster-surfing for a full hour in the murky depths of the malodorous metal bin behind the Heavenly Bamboo Restaurant when he came upon the prize that would portend his future, a soy-stained plastic container holding a single unblemished fortune cookie.

—*Rosemary Dunne*
Amherst, Virginia

He etched paper with his pen, carving each word in every sentence like a fine wood-craftsman creating a model ship through the narrow neck of a bottle, building paragraphs to scale like miniature hulls with all their embellishments—port windows, anchors and chains, rounded bolt-heads, the occasional barnacle—topping off chapters with a majestic superstructure of gun turrets, antennas and radar dishes, like a finely honed *Bismarck* poised for massive broadsides in the vicious and salty ocean, but, unable to sustain war-readiness, his hand numbed, he began writing with a soft porosity, like a block of whittled balsa bobbing in a mud puddle, realizing at the same time the inevitable historic fate of the battleship he had created and the problem he faced in retracting his swollen hand through the bottleneck.

—*John P. Doucet*
Raceland, Louisiana

Brenda Malthwit: attorney at law, young, attractive, well educated, and full of self-confidence; a woman who, as swiftly as her lascivious male coworkers undressed her with their eyes, would mentally fold the clothes neatly and put them in a pile.

—*Rick Vetter*
Riverside, California

Call me Ishma . . . Bob.   —*Charles Smith*
                                        Kitty Hawk, North Carolina

When the gigantic sunflower was bowled over by the blazing fast ball, the crowd of overzealous hobgoblins, in a frenzied rush of . . . no, this isn't working out.

—*Tyler Mays*
Redmond, Washington

We had been married long enough for Fifi's burning gaze and flaring nostrils to tell me *exactly* what she wanted, so I hurriedly peeled off her tight satin dress, with a flick of the wrist dispatched her lacy French brassiere, with practiced precision made a "ringer" with her garter belt on the furthest bedpost, and as I sent her imported silk stockings arcing gracefully into the laundry hamper, I dropped to my knees and promised never, *never* to go into town wearing her clothes again.   —*Wm. W. "Buddy" Ocheltree*
Port Townsend, Washington

Jackson was just the kind of guy your mother told you about and your father warned you about, but when your mother told you it was like, "Wow, I knew this guy back in college who was so cool . . ." and when your Dad told you, it was more like, "You take it from me, young lady, if I ever catch you with a guy like that—'cause I was one of 'em myself once . . ." and you're like, "Oh, right, I'm sure . . ."

—*F. Shaw-Brabazon*
Hensonville, New York

The sad tale of how I came to be a narcissist with sadistic and dictatorial tendencies may bore you, but I feel like

ranting and will spit bullets if ignored; so sit down, shut up, and read.
—*Verna Jordan*
Owen Sound, Ontario

"What a difference a day makes"—well, that was a mouthful, thought Jennifer Jasmine as she looked into the lumpy bowl of oatmeal that Ruth Anne had just put in front of her, just one little day—that's all it had taken to turn her life upside down like so many pineapple slices staring up at you with those big cherry eyes all floating in a brown-sugar-and-butter mess that was not so much different from the mess she had managed to get herself into, in just "twenty-four little hours."
—*Michele M. Ferrier*
San Francisco, California

She weighed 320 and wanted me to be her personal trainer, but all I could think was that, of all the gym joints in all the towns in all the world, she had to walk into mine.
—*David Stone*
Mt. Airy, North Carolina

"By Myself, this sentence belongs in the Bulwer-Lytton Contest!" said Jupiter jovially.
—*Michael J. Saxton*
Davis, California

Our story begins with Abe's first cry, issuing from the homely log cabin where he was born—a cabin surrounded by daffodils, many in bloom, but some stunted or even dying from the attacks of the echidna snail, a pest brought North in the bowels of a carthorse drawing a snake-oil salesman from Tallahassee, whose guaranteed cure for dropsy did little for the disease, but was so rich in alcohol

as to leave the patient blissfully uncaring, while her money
. . . but I digress.
—*David Arthur Johnson*
Honolulu, Hawaii

Carrying by the nape of its neck the erswhile pet whose
claws had shredded her newly upholstered sofa and whose
bowels had soiled her new rug, which offenses her twisted
mind said could be expiated only on the guillotine, a furious Madame Robespierre stormed into the conference
room of the Directory where now presided her loathed
and feared husband Jacques Robespierre—Robespierre!
the architect and chief enforcer of the infamous Reign of
Terror that left wives widows, children fatherless, parents
childless, pets masterless, and Sindey Carton headless;
Robespierre! the heads of whose victims rested in every
bloody basket of wheat-, barley-, and even oat-bran in
France; at the mercy of this of-like-mind-to-hers, merci-
less fiend in human form did Madame Robespierre leave
the life and hopes of poor, insufficiently housebroken
Whiskers, the Robespierre household cat.
—*Zalman Gaibel*
Chicago, Illinois

Victor emerged from the house in his sinew-enhancing
Spandex body suit, donned his speed racing helmet and
calfskin cycling gloves, straddled his 12-speed Road
Warrior model 300D with its carbon-magnesium alloy
frame, electric-assisted derailleur, tiger grip touring tires,
and recurved handle bars reminiscent of the horns of a
Miura fighting bull—and emasculated himself on the bicy-
cle seat.
—*Larry Ward*
Midland, Michigan

Igor was reluctant to put his muddy boot against the white but slowly reddening tunic of a fellow soldier, but how else could he extract his bayonet?

—*John M. Gilbert, Sr.*
Branford, Florida

Harry tangled his fingers in her matted mane, forcing her head back down to the water— "just like drowning a kitten," he told himself, "like a kitty cat drowning"—but he wondered if it might not have been easier just to shoot the old mare.
—*Michael Fleeman*
Blue Ridge, Georgia

THE
FRIGID
NORTHERN
WIND
HOWLED . . .

FROM *It Was a Dark and Stormy Night: The Final Conflict* (1992)

"It was the eve of the yearly whale-slaughtering festival," thought Mamook as her horny fingers relentlessly pushed the whalebone needle through the sole of the mukluk; and suddenly, unaccountably, she began to blubber.

—*Debra Yoo Hessemer*
Chicago, Illinois

Fierce, icy winds mercilessly whipped the naked trees into splinters and sent birds wheeling into the horizon as Nick Savage mushed his heavy sled on through the blinding whiteness; next time, he thought wearily, I'm hooking up the dogs.

—*Leann Roberts*
Iron Station, North Carolina

The frigid northern wind howled and poked an icy finger up Strom Romberg's fur-lined parka as he bent solicitously over his lead sled-dog, Shasta, who, responding to the she-wolf's siren call the night before, had slipped his rawhide lead and romped all night in the forest, returning at dawn exhausted and with all the hair on the inside of his thighs rubbed off, but then, as Strom sagely remarked to his stalwart native companion Ee-wo Kluk, "Doesn't everyone?"

—*Simone Ostrander*
Sanger, California

"Without fresh underwear," Father Louis was saying, drooling madly now, his hands chopping at unseen barbarian hordes, lipstick smeared across his chest and neck, a stack of chairs seventy-feet high teetering directly behind him, the cast of *Gilligan's Island* chanting the words *ptarmigan* to his left, "a man is nothing, an animal—I spit on such a man."

—*Charles Howland*
St. Paul, Minnesota

It was one of those amorphous, lightless Arctic days when the seamless gray sky meets the unfriendly grayer waters somewhere at a boundless horizon and the wind hurls little stiletto ice crystals at unprotected flesh; the featureless landscape broken by only one object, the silhouette of Nanook hunkered down next to a blowhole as he had been for the last twelve hours, harpoon angled ever so effortlessly over the hole, squatting there like a tundra gargoyle ever so motionless . . . motionless, dead and frozen solid as a forgotten package of fish sticks in the back of a refrigerator freezer compartment.

—*Rick Vetter*
Riverside, California

Alexis pushed the button for the twenty-ninth floor and, oblivious to the fact that the strange old man behind her was wearing a cape and racquetball goggles, began the first leg of a great adventure that would eventually leave her in a motel room just outside of Reno with nothing but a jar of pickles and a pocket full of toothpicks to defend herself from the attacking guerrilla soldiers.

—*Diona Linardo*
Las Vegas, Nevada

Snap, crash, bang! went the mast as it toppled deckward toward the helpless boatswain, causing his whole life to flash before his eyes, leaving out of course his infancy and those parts where he was very drunk or asleep.

—*Eric F. Bam*
New York, New York

As the finely honed points of the magnificent bull elk's antlers perforated his spleen, lungs, and lower colon, Lenny the Grifter wished he had stayed working the streets in Times Square instead of going up to the Rockies where this dumb animal had figured out that three-card monte was a con, and gored him.   —*Richard Patching*
Calgary, Alberta

Sir Roderick squatted awkwardly in the bleak Sahara landscape and reflected that it was easier for a rich man to ride a camel through the eye of a needle and trot merrily off to the kingdom of heaven than it was for an Englishman to pass a fortnight's worth of Moroccan couscous through his digestive tract.   —*Lindy Tilp*
Long Island, New York

Leaping buildings at a single bound is a piece of cake; being faster than a speeding bullet is no sweat; and acting like a mild mannered reporter at a great metropolitan newspaper I can do with my eyes closed—but having to stuff this damn cape inside this lousy shirt is starting to get on my nerves, he thought, exiting his favorite telephone booth.   —*Mike Sturman*
Beaumont, California

Shielding his frostbitten face from the knife-like Himalayan downdraft, secret agent Biff Rockley braced his muscular frame on the bleak, narrow ledge, knocked the ice grimly from his left piton, and, shifting his back-pack, felt compulsively for the reassuringly soft bulk of the strychnine-laced raisin kugel which Swiss intelligence had specially prepared for the Dali Lama's brother-in-law, reflecting bitterly, "I hope to cripes we didn't get a bum steer from that thieving Turkish dental hygienist."

—*Rich Clancey*
Brookline, Massachusetts

"There is little to be thankful for," thought Frank, his wife having been taken hostage at the French embassy, "but at least I've got my health," and with that he stubbed out his cigarette and put the empty fifth of scotch in the recyclables bin.

—*Mark Watson*
Cary, North Carolina

When he heard the desperate voice over the intercom of flight 467, "If there is an ichthyologist on board, would he please come to the flight deck?" he smiled, left his seat (2B), and went upstairs to the cockpit of the 747 where the desperate flight attendant was saying, "We need a doctor as well," to which he replied, "Harvard Med '73!" . . . "and a pilot,"— "multiengine commercial qualified"— "Thank God!"— "No, thank Allah, for this remarkable series of coincidences is a sign and you are my hostages; we're going to Algiers," but they did not, since, for all his other skills, Abdul Salim was not trained in navigation and our tale commences in Oslo.

—*Donald deKieffer*
Washington, D.C.

Many years later, as he faced the firing squad, he thought back to that cold winter morning so many years

before, when he had faced that other firing squad, and he was suddenly seized with the irrational hope that these were the same guys.   —M. J. Hayward-Ambrose
                                        Seattle, Washington

"Baaaaaaaaaad man, you're a baaaaaaaaaad man!—but your cleaver cannot harm me for my coat is a wool of steel!" bleated Supersheep as he deftly butted the weapon out of the pudgy hand of his arch-enemy Myron Metger and subdued the chubby butcher with a lightning-quick chop to the side of his meaty face, and as his stunned attacker lay squealing at his hooves, the ovine avenger, his powerful forelegs akimbo and his black-and-white cashmere cape billowing heroically in the breeze, admonished, "Now I've gotta lam, but remember: The wheel of crime spins tatty wool," and as he waddled mightily back to his thankful flock, he realized that his greatest adventure was just beginning.   —Dan Braverman
                                        Houston, Texas

Jack Meade stood six-feet, five-inches tall, weighed two-hundred and fifty pounds, had lettered in three sports in high school and college, spoke five languages, had earned four martial arts black belts, could press a quarter of a ton, maintained qualifications with every small-arms weapon available to the Department of Defense, and made an excellent leader for the Delta Force unit under his command, but unfortunately he had slipped in the shower and fractured his skull the morning of the mission, so I was called up from administrative services to take his place.   —P. F. Bruns
                                        Wahiawa, Hawaii

The old man removed his pipe to shoot a pebble of phlegm expertly into a distant cuspidor before continuing his tale: "Aye," he whispered darkly, "things was diffrint then, what with the groilin' storms, the creakin' timbers, and the forkin' lightnin' asplittin' of the mizzenbockets like matchwood; and men's muscles torn wi' the weight o' the catch, and the fish amoilin' and ascreelin' in the nets— and them albertrosses, thick as gulls, adarkenin' of the sky with their wingspans and with their evil beaks snappin' fingers off of young lads, and us too affeared to harpoon the beggars owin' to Neptune's curse; and all the toim the Sea, the broodin' Sea, awaitin' and awatchin' to drag us agaggin' and apukin' into the bottomless bellies of its denizens."
                                                        —*Gina Williams*
                                                        Talybont, Wales

"Call me Ish—waaaaaach!" whooped my pale-faced fellow voyager, clinging miserably to the *Pequod*'s weather rail and ralfing like the landlubber he was.
                                                        —*Richard Raymond III*
                                                        Roanoke, Virginia

The fearsome beast slowly turned its repulsive head and focused its malevolent gaze upon heroic Ralph the Barbarian, freezing his blood with terror, turning his heart to ice, and halting his breathing, which, of course, killed him.
                                                        —*Alexander J. Edmonds*
                                                        Blackburn, Australia

FABIO HAD
EVERYTHING
MARISSA
HAD EVER
DREAMED
OF IN A
MAN . . .

"In the wan light of the Biloxi dawn, Cytheraea lay crumpled on the trundle bed like so much used Kleenex, or perhaps like the sticky remnants of a box of Cap'n Crunch cereal that someone has dumped out, callously and without any regard for his mother's feelings after she cleaned the kitchen, in order to get the free prize inside, your honor."

—*Charles Dodt*
Concord, California

Fabio had everything Marissa had ever dreamed of in a man: the face of Adonis, the body of Hercules, and the I.Q. of a Thompson Seedless grape.

—*Penny Lee Ellsworth*
Salinas, California

Disregarding the snarling Rottweilers tearing at his now dismembered limb, Lord Craventlow staggered toward the mausoleum, crying out derangedly in grief for Elspeth as the governess Dora Maude Whrat, out picking wildflowers to press in her heavily annotated diary, stepped discreetly behind a cypress and bit her fist in tearful empathy.

—*Lindy Tilp*
Long Island, New York

"Babs, you is my woman now!" cried Thor, the skimpily clad Scandinavian stud-muffin as he ripped open Barbara's lace bodice with his pearly meat-mashers, defiantly tossed back the lusty, leonine mane that rendered him unemployable in ninety percent of the job market, and pierced her soul with his azure peepers (bluer than a Berber's family jewels, those weepers!), then flexing a few major gladiator's muscles (muscles that almost yelped, "I am narcissistic enough to exercise fourteen hours a day!"), before he savagely thrust her upon the canopy bed with such force that the silk sheets trembled in anticipation of forbidden love; yet our heroine, the fiercely independent (though vulnerable) Barbara Cartland, merely rolled her eyes, yawned, and thought, "Ye gads! what won't these Fabio wanna-bes do to get written into a romance novel?"
—*Margaret Ellen Fiske*
Omaha, Nebraska

With her husband's body sprawled across one half of the bed and Maggie, the monstrous mastiff occupying the other, Polly Pauline Featheringame had no other option but to curl up in the extra-large, cedar-scented, and heavily haired-over L.L. Bean dog nest. —*Geri Davis*
Prescott, Arizona

The room fell to a hush as the divine Countess Caroline "of Bruxelberry" Smith delicately, smoothly trickled down the steps of the ballroom like a huge blob of butterscotch, or possibly pistachio pudding spit onto a stained-glass window and left to slither down on its own, except that Caroline had much more hair and looked a heckuva lot better in a bodice. —*Jennifer S. Anderson*
San Jose, California

She saw him coming through the rye, bringing in the sheaves, this towering silo of a man, his skin aglow with a tan of catfish-fried perfection whose cornflower blue eyes sought her out, drawing her near until she felt like laughing spring rain, racing into his arms where she raked her harvest-wearied hands through his straw-flecked hair and, kissing his furrowed brow, muttered, "You've come home, John dear, you've come home." —*Gini Jones*
Santa Fe, New Mexico

She felt the disappointment wash right through her, purging her like so much greasy dishwater swirling down a drain, carrying away the remains of a once fine dinner, as she coughed into a tissue before wiping haphazardly at her face in an awkward attempt to hide the salty tears that had escaped unbidden through her eyelids, bypassing her body's other flush systems. —*Mary Ann Gieszelmann*
Roseville, California

Monica thrashed about on the bed, her breaths coming fitfully, like a whipped dog approaching his cruel master's outstretched hand, and as the first rays of dawn's golden light broke through the tattered, faded curtains of her bedroom window, she realized despairingly, achingly, that there would be no sleep for her, not with the memory of Basil's sensuous lips haunting her fevered dreams, and all that damn light streaming in through the window.
—*Barbara J. Loera*
Austin, Texas

I should have bolted out the garage door before she pulled her platinum head out from under the hood of that two-tone peach road boat at which she was swearing a blue streak, before she wiped her grease-blackened hands slowly across the protruding front bumpers of her tight gun-metal-gray coveralls, before the slippery green smell of her forty-weight perfume pinked my nose, but I didn't go yellow and she purpled me for it big time, shifting her weight on the fly and wrenching me out of my tired brown shoes with an unsignaled right like a big chrome-plated four-eighty-four block swung by a junk yard crane.

—*Matthew Levesque*
Alameda, California

The ravishingly beautiful Lady Latrishia's astonishing milk-white, blue-veined bosom heaved magnificently as she sighed soulfully while reclining in a near-swoon on her silky pink, satin, flower-embroidered boudoir chaise, and contemplated her sad fate at the mercy of the *haute monde* if her recent foolish romp in the castle maze became the latest *on dit* for the snickering snobs in the Pump Room at Bath, as, indeed, it would, if that odious fop, Lord Neether Nohrkinstop, tattled the least tidbit of the shockingly cant converse she had exchanged with the dashing rake, Baronet Freddie Fustaine—who already regarded her as the merest twittering ninnyhammer—and so she had to wait, for, alas, one can't recant cant, can one?

—*Marguerite R. Clark*
Fresno, California

Last night I dreamt I went to Manderly again, which was quite odd considering that I was already *at* Manderly, and that the main theme of my dream concerned a dozen Star Fleet officers cavorting out of uniform on a beach on Alpha Centauri V. —*Anthony Buckland*
North Vancouver, British Columbia

Lying beside the dozing Baron in the morning mist, which was more like a fog this time—and dank—suffused with satisfaction, sated with sensation, and aswim with sweat, I silently hung a "no vacancy" sign over the hotel of my heart.   —*Sallie Baldwin*
Greenwich, Connecticut

"Different worlds be damned!" he thought, gazing down raptly at the silken head nestled so trustingly against his muscular shoulder, her femininity a feather's pressure against the rock-hard physique which bespoke his twin devotions to hard work and hard play and yet his legacy as well, a gift from the gods which also included among the styrofoam peanuts of the cosmos thick, curling hair, intelligence, and charm; remembering his haughty family's ill-concealed horror as they met Caroline and beheld his lowborn love's inherent dignity and fiercely independent mien, he uttered a low bark of laughter, whereupon Caroline awoke from her nap, stretched lazily, bestowed a moist kisslet on his patrician jaw, extended a shapely leg in a motion so graceful it would have thrilled a balletomane carved of solid granite, which he certainly was not, and proceeded to lick herself most delicately, an entirely appropriate action for the uncrowned princess of the alley-cat universe, thereby making him, at least for the moment, quite possibly the happiest Irish wolfhound on earth.
—*Melinda Chilton Dickinson*
Birmingham, Alabama

She shunned him utterly, for their hearts forked like swamp and stable, and though a mare may at times go astray, delighting the crocs with which the DeWilds stocked their grounds, yet, *was* Miss Millicent Favorhorst, the new governess, such a goose? young Werther was forced to wonder, as he squatted simian-like in the front parlor slurping on his earlobe, which hung exceedingly low, and gazed at her well-rounded bosom, which did not.

—*D. L. Armstrong*
Long Beach, California

"I like my men the way I like my brownies," Nicole said as she stared deeply into his big brown bedroom eyes, "thick and firm; dense, but yielding to the touch; and with a fresh but not overpowering odor you want to stick your face in."

—*Amy Cohen*
New York, New York

The Way We Live Now: From E-Mail to E. Coli

I was a fifty-four-year-old male virgin but I'm all right now.
—*Arden Ohl*
Modesto, California

Kablam! and all Marvin's ingenious plans went up in smoke, as did Marvin himself, in that terrible moment when he learned that you can't send a letter bomb by e-mail.
—*Brian Holmes*
San Jose, California

"I run out of Prozac on Wednesday . . . that's tomorrow," and it was with those words that, at last, veteran employee Brian had the entire east wing of the post office to himself.
—*Kent D. Glienke*
Oak Park, Illinois

A brain tumor had made Montigue so psychotic that he swore to kill the first human being who said hello to him or even looked him in the eye, but he never did, living the last six months of his life in New York City.

—*Ben. T. Young*
Tempe, Arizona

Usually, Malcolm enjoyed his leisurely, late-night stroll through Central Park, where the stillness soothed his ner-

vous nature—however, this time was different because, looking through his small, horned-rim glasses, he saw three extremely large men walking down the path toward him, all acting rather rambunctious, one carrying a forty-pound ghetto blaster on his shoulder, another playing viciously with a three-foot length of chain while the third man sang loud profane lyrics to the music, at which point Malcolm said irritably, "Gentlemen, you will have to turn down the radio—it annoys me!"   —*Charles DeLongfield*
Kelseyville, California

The gopher incident behind him now, Dennis raised his fists triumphantly and told the roaring crowd, most of whom were staggeringly drunk on the bathtub gin he had set out in troughs in front of the stage, "There'll be plenty of eggs in Boise!" yet he was unable to dispel the image of his estranged wife, Helen, her wrists and ankles festooned with Post-it notes inscribed with Dorothy Parker witticisms, dancing the limbo with her precious Greek auto mechanic.   —*Charles Howland*
St. Paul, Minnesota

As his spindly gray cat, Harley, idly licked a sticky abscess while perched atop the rusting chopper's cracked leather seat, Hogface hoisted the heavy NFL tumbler of foamy Olde DownTowne Stout from the greasy porch table in a toast to another smog-fried L.A. sunset, and, as he did so, mounting pressure percolated up from deep inside his bare tattooed belly; and the ensuing belch, bellowing off the porch's dusty stucco walls like claps of angry thunder, launched Harley into a parabolic eighth-life flight clean through the old bike's chromed handlebar goal posts,

over its blinded headlamp, and straight into Professor Peabody's primly pruned privet hedge. —*Jerry L. Boal*
Corvallis, Oregon

The clarinet player was sending some smooth, deep tones through his licorice stick, the guitarist was making the strings come alive, and the drummer was beating those skins as though his life depended on it, and then there was me, an out-of-work carpenter wondering if the stripper needed any shelves built. —*Mike Sturman*
Beaumont, California

The dirty gray sky hung over the city like the sneeze shield on God's salad bar, soot snaking up from the smoke stacks below like the greasy fingers of some snot-nosed brat who just has to leave his fingerprints suspended over the cauliflower, and Jake watched from his grimy window, cursing the city that, to him, was just so much of God's broccoli and carrot medley in light hollandaise, which he, like the former President, just couldn't stomach anymore.
—*Robert Hugh Brown*
Naples, Florida

Crusty old Tom Cruickshank bundled packets of oatmeal, rice, biscuits, Weetbix; clattered cans of tomatoes, prawns, cocktail frankfurters, mushrooms, pressed ham, beets; crashed jars of marmalade, honey, minced coriander; crushed plastic bags of vermicelli, potato chips, nuts, and breadrolls into the pit of his supermarket shopping cart, all the time wondering why food had replaced sex as the major theme in modern American movies.
—*Garth Madsen*
Frankston, Australia

"Freeways—yes, the 101 is so baroque, or is it Freudian, with, like, those tunnels, or I guess that's the Pasadena— but the 405 interchange with the Santa Monica at about 4:30 in the afternoon in a Honda Civic with Oingo-Boingo on, like *blasting*, is so *being there*," Jessie bubbled soulfully.
—*Sandra M. Jensen*
Eugene, Oregon

As the city came into view, Kim pressed her face to the car window, a look of utter excitement and expectation in her eyes, a look that might have graced Columbus' face at the sight of the New World, or Dorothy's when she finally reached Oz, except that Kim was coming to South Bend, Indiana, and, although she didn't know it, the excitement in her life was over for good.   —*Stephen Allen*
South Bend, Indiana

With a loud pop from the steaming contents of the microwave, Sara discovered the similarities beween the Chinese take out and pet store hamster cartons.
—*Bradley Loeding*
Bellevue, Washington

The dark and stormy night was past, and long, gray fingers of translucent fog crept through the open window, over dusty venetian blinds (the wide ones, installed sometime early during the Hoover administration), and across the cracked and peeling mud-covered linoleum to the rusty iron single bed where Nadine tossed fitfully, trying to avoid coming to grips with the new day, a day in which she must face the unalterable fact that Rupert, her lukewarm (due mostly to a chronic prostate condition, but aggravated by her bad breath) lover of twenty-three years,

had abruptly abandoned both her and his long-term job as bag boy at Charlie's Market to take up with some young chick who lived in a yurt in the foothills of life and raised spitting llamas and guinea fowl and was trying to make a go of subsistence farming without the use of pesticides; that, and the fact that she had wasted twenty-three years eating salad and cottage cheese. —*Kathleen Wynveen*
Sheboygan Falls, Wisconsin

L. L. Fauntleroy wasn't having *half* the retail success he'd envisioned when fate landed him in Freeport, Maine, with a boatload of ruffled shirts and, frankly, rather silly blue satin knee britches, so he changed his name to Bean, went New England butch, and the rest is, well, you know . . . —*Susan Bird Freund*
Charlottesville, Virginia

Steven couldn't be sure, as he heard the landing gear rumble open beneath his seat and gazed out at the landing field, its illuminated runways strangely elegant in the summer evening, whether his stomachache had been caused by the turbulence over Venezuela, the cheap and undercooked airline food, or the fourteen heroin-filled parakeets stuffed in condoms he had swallowed in the La Paz terminal men's room. —*Frank M. Carrano*
Branford, Connecticut

Four small words added almost as an afterthought to his order at the neighborhood Jack-in-the-Box restaurant were to change Jeremy's life forever: "and make it rare."
—*Tim Fuller*
Chehalis, Washington

LYTTONY
II

"**G**od, I'm tired," thought Jim-Bob as he jammed the seventeen-speed road ranger into double-compound fifth gear and gracefully swung the big rig into the right lane, effortlessly flattening the front end of a '69 LTD and making it resemble a giant green metallic spatula with wheels on the handle.
—*T. L. Bulgrin*
Owen, Wisconsin

"Blammo, you bad, bad little monkey!" exclaimed Clevenger in exasperation at the simian who had just jumped from his shoulder, grabbed the policeman's service revolver, fired four shots into the President of the United States as he passed in a motorcade, and then put the still-smoking gun into Clevenger's hand and scampered off unseen into the crowd, which now faced him angrily.
—*John F. Browning*
Flemington, New Jersey

Maude, regrettably, was a few Styrofoam cups short of a landfill.
—*Rev. William F. Charles*
Cassopolis, Michigan

The main problem with being a vampire in old New Orleans was disease: drink the blood of a victim every day

and you were immortal; drink the blood of a victim with tertian malaria and you risked being immortal with chills and fever every forty-eight hours, until the end of the world.
— *Michael J. Saxton*
Davis, California

In his prime, sportswriters say, the legendary Muhammad Ali could float like a butterfly and sting like a bee; however, only the trusted insiders who merited invitations to his post-fight cocktail parties ever got a sampling of his lesser-known wildlife impressions: Ali could cluck like a chicken, bray like a burro, waddle like a penguin, squeal like a pig, croak like a tree frog, ball up like a sowbug, flap his arms like a fruitbat, wiggle his ears like a dingo, crawl on his belly like a gila monster, and bellow like a six-hundred-pound Alaskan harbor seal in heat.
— *Brian D. Smith*
New Whiteland, Indiana

Lester closed the thick anthology of horror stories he was reading as the clock chimed the midnight hour, and thought to himself, *Why is it that people are such absolute idiots in horror stories . . . can't they see what's behind the . . .* when there was a heavy thumping at the front door, so he tossed the book aside, got up from his comfortable chair in front of the warm, cozy fire and went to the door, wondering, *Who can that be?*
— *Thomas Erik Nielsen*
Sonoma, California

Remember this, foolish mortals, when ye stare headlong into the mind-paralyzing void, the inky black nothingness of existence, the hellish yawning maw of the abyss—it's

pretty damn dark, so give it a few minutes for your eyes to adjust.
—*Frank M. Carrano*
Branford, Connecticut

The need to, say, know, and the need to say no are not as similar as they may sound, and it was Madame Korbynski's failure to distinguish the two on that swelter-ing summer night in Prague that resulted in the birth of the famous linguist who would damn well never let the rest of us forget to make this and even finer distinctions.
—*Jim Terr*
Santa Fe, New Mexico

Now that she was mature, and both of her eyes were on the same side of her head, Hortense knew she could land a rich old flounder who'd take her right to the bottom, where the sand was soft, the light was dim, and food just crawled right into your mouth.
—*Linda Needham*
Hillsboro, Oregon

Some believe there is no limit to human depravity, but that's not what Grover McCormack was thinking as he pre-pared to amass and eventually display the largest collec-tion of Wayne Newton recordings that Greenland had ever seen.
—*Benjamin Lichtman*
Laguna Hills, California

As the previous patient passed him by, holding a newly blood-soaked handkerchief over his mouth, Michael knew he had probably picked the wrong psychiatrist to help him with his masochism; he smiled guiltily to himself.
—*P. F. Bruns*
Wahiawa, Hawaii

A twinkle—a very faint twinkle but a twinkle still, which you could just see if you looked carefully into the slit between the old man's lids—lit, or at least softened, his rheumy old eyes as he tapped his pipe on the china bowl with a practiced knock just hard enough to dislodge a rank, steamy, sodden cud of fool tobacco, but not hard enough to chip the china or mar the briar, and started what was at once the most incredible and moving tale I had ever heard, if you don't count stuff like Edgar Allan Poe or the Bible.

—*Eric F. Bam*
New York, New York

Theresa lunged for the salad fork and hurled it at Claude, a chain-smoking taxidermist with whom she had been discussing the history of lemonade for the past seven hours, in a move which both alarmed and intrigued Patrick, her husband and luge coach, unaccountably causing him to recall his childhood in Bali, where his father, a bee-keeper and part-time leprechaun, would pay obese violinists to dance naked among the palms. —*Charles Howland*
St. Paul, Minnesota

As the first pale pink edgings of dawn blushed the eastern horizon while the rest of the sky was black still and, oh, the stars! his weathered hand gripped one of the two long wooden rails held parallel by a series of short, evenly spaced rungs, and he thought, "This is a ladder."

—*Bob Annechino*
Rochester, New York

Belvedere paused with Angelica's bedroom door slightly ajar, and cautiously stuck his head into the great hall, hearing ever so faintly the screams and groans of the

doomed souls below in the damp, rat-infested, iron-clad cells, then scurried, knock-kneed, to the water closet.
—*Gus D. Ralph*
Sacramento, California

He reached out hungrily, caressing her soft, squeezable skin, which, although browner than café au lait, seemed to him a perfect hue, and cried to himself as he imagined her syrupy voice beseeching him to taste the ever-flowing honey-sweet discharge that issued from the hole in the top of her skull—oh, how he loved Mrs. Butterworth!
—*Jeff Richards*
West Valley City, Utah

Carl had never dreamed of killing his parents, not until the day he tried to show them how to operate the timer on the new VCR.
—*John Grundmann*
Bethpage, New York

"Why does a dried apricot in a puddle of White-Out so closely resemble a fried egg?" he wondered as he licked the little brush.
—*Julie S. Ponsford*
Sacramento, California

"You have a dirty mouth," she sneered, and I thought to myself, "Sure, but who wouldn't after exhuming himself from a premature grave with the sleeves of his burial suit still sewn to the lapels?"
—*Anthony Buckland*
North Vancouver, British Columbia

IN DUBIOUS
TASTE

FROM *Son of "It Was a Dark and Stormy Night"* (1986)

As she looked down at the battered and bloodied body before her, Grace felt a little disappointed in herself for having so brutally beaten Bobby Meyer to death, but even after thirty-two years of teaching, the one thing she had never quite learned to tolerate was a student who picked his nose and then ate it.

—*Rose Mary Gergick*
Tonganoxie, Kansas

As the sun slowly rose in the east (causing the dawn light to be lost), as the crew's tempers subsequently rose, and as the bottom of her swimsuit inexorably rode up, Kathy Ireland pondered whether modeling thong bikinis for *Sports Illustrated* was all it was cracked up to be.

—*Thomas Weisgerber*
Saginaw, Michigan

The day he left the army, John's discharge was both honorable and cottage cheese–like.

—*Michael David Edwards*
Everett, Washington

The unfortunate amount of slack in his bikini underwear amply attested to the emotional emptiness of his love

life, Bernard reflected, as he adjusted his hairpiece to the left and himself to the right. —*Terrence O. Carroll*
San Jose, California

Proud were the firm, upright breasts, flaring nostrils, and sinewy forearms of Alexandra Keller, though she was no relation to Helen, as she was quick to point out to everybody. —*Jane Dioguardi Plantz*
Meriden, Connecticut

The tombs held their secrets like so many dusty bus station lockers or the fetid panels at peep shows where Balthazar Bogenbogen drooled quietly, dreaming of plunging a throbbing saber saw into the chest of yet another unsuspecting victim, and his wretched eyes illuminated like fireflies on the moist August nights that littered the memories of his idyllic childhood. —*Jim Stein*
Allentown, Pennsylvania

She was as cheap as a grocery store gumball, as easy to make as an instant chocolate pudding, as tempting as a triple-chocolate sundae with whipped cream at a Weight Watchers weigh-in, and as hot as the fillings in those pies you get at the fast food places that have warnings on the box that say, "Warning: Filling may be hot!" but before Frank Furter could ravage her like a senior citizen at a half-price, all-you-can-eat buffet, she was off like a prom dress. —*Carol I. Cohen*
Temple Terrace, Florida

"Perhaps it would be better if you stopped seeing me," said the self-pity-ridden Gunther before he blinded his very surprised lover with the poker. —*Caitlin Shirts*
Provo, Utah

Although she tried for hours to arrange the cattails artistically, Sara could never quite figure out what to do with the tiny paws that drooped over the edge of the vase.

—*Bill Robinson*
Canal Fulton, Ohio

There are few sights sadder than an orphanage on Christmas morning; unfortunately, one of them is a nursing home into which a fully-loaded and fully-fueled jumbo jet has just crashed, so you can imagine that nobody in Hook and Ladder Company 14 was very cheerful on the ride back to the station.   —*Robert D. Norris, Jr.*
Tulsa, Oklahoma

The bug-encrusted light bulb barely illuminated a woman's face that might, for once, be honest, but the face swayed on a lean neck rising from bony shoulders, part of an unpadded body (the shoulders were just a taste of bone-clacking to come) sheathed in synthetic silky stuff, sort of like a condom on a tree branch.   —*Cindy Robinson*
Knoxville, Tennessee

The shimmering droplets coursing down the window pane were as wet and copious as the tears clouding Rebecca's vision, and the similarities did not end there—for both the window frame and her lovely lashes were rimmed in red, and the pane, like her left eyeball, was glass.

—*Tony Stoltzfus*
Goshen, Indiana

Gladys was an insomniac with a bladder problem, but despite her well-designed attempts to get some shut-eye, she was still pissing away her sleeping time.

—*Jennifer L. Rosen*
New York, New York

"All living things excrete," rhapsodized Professor Wilkinson, "from the oxygen and CO_2 given off by green plants to the honeydew of aphids, from the tarry specks of stable flies to the delightful knobby keg-shaped frass of tobacco hornworms—the tenuous hyphenated lines trailing out from your tropical fish—the dry round day pellets and the moist, grape-cluster night pellets of rabbits—ah, but today, class, we're going to discuss *canis domestica*, and when you're talking dogs, ladies and gentlemen, you're talking Tootsie Rolls."
                                        —*Cynthia Conyers*
                                   Warner Springs, California

Futilely jabbing at the doze button of her incessantly ringing biological clock, Celeste unwillingly awoke to a brilliant summer morning, the sky unmarred by atmospheric flocculation, save one lone brown cloud, looking for all the world like a skid mark on the underwear of heaven.
                                        —*Linda Chalker-Scott*
                                          Hamburg, New York

Entering his large, book-lined study on the second floor of the re-created Romanesque family mansion on the banks of the Hudson River, Signore del Cadzione crossed to the expensive oak desk that commanded the space beneath the leaded stained-glass window that a forefather had salvaged from a crumbling monastery in the northwest corner of Lombardy, his aristocratic profile gently defined by the stained glass, his strong, yet slender manicured fingers lifting the lid of the velvet-lined box and, gently removing the anniversary gift from his wife and companion of thirty-eight years—a handsomely tooled, silver-butted .38 caliber revolver that had been coaxed from the private collection of Count Balzini—he thought to him-

self, "Geez, I bet I could shoot the nits off a gnat's nuts at thoity feet wid dis!"
—*George A. Gordon*
Nepean, Ontario

"Gee, it's great to get back into this again!" exclaimed Dr. Kot, a part-time proctologist, as he rose from his stool to clap a dollop of Vaseline onto the patient's protruding backside.
—*Barrett Kalellis*
Pinckney, Michigan

With the birds chirping mellifluously and the sun sharing her warmth generously while the sky cloaked the earth in brilliant blue, in a storybook-like castle by a crystal clear brook, deep in the emerald green forest, Sir Reginald discovered blood in his stool.
—*Michael David Edwards*
Everett, Washington

As the windows began getting foggy, Elizabeth lay back in the dark, musty backseat of the Ford and wondered, "Am I getting too old to let Ricky play 'Taxi, Taxi, how much is your fare?' "
—*Gregg Florence*
Cerritos, California

Raven-haired Countess Montessa, whose beauty, wit, charm, and vivacity were legendary throughout the realm, reflected pensively on the quirk of fate that had sent her to this bleak tower of banishment, and relieving her boredom she practiced tootling her scales, beginning with the lower, more resonant octaves, for equally legendary were her frequent attacks of flatulence.

—*Carolyn Brittain*
Sand Springs, Oklahoma

What began as a casual scratch of the nose for Eugene Poindexter quickly evolved into a definite pick and then rapidly a mining expedition whereby he inadvertently pinched his pituitary gland and, nine years later, became the Pittsburgh Steeler's star fullback.

—*Jim "Quasimofo" Sheppeck*
Irvine, California

He was certainly an attractive, well-rounded child, yet he shrank away from the other boys; hanging out with Sophocles, Hercules, Damocles, and Heracles, somehow, Testicles just felt *different*.   —*K. P. Stone*
Cambridge, Massachusetts

"It looks as though the king aced the queen," Jack Tenn mused with a straight face as he inspected the previously unpublished photograph of the late (or is he?) Elvis Presley playing tennis with Elizabeth II, poring over the picture with the keen, unfaltering eye of a teenage boy watching his cheerleader girlfriend unhook her bra for the first time in the backseat of his father's El Dorado.

—*Jeff Richards*
West Valley City, Utah

After battling a bout of diarrhea for a week, Steve was wiped out.   —*Jeff Ottney*
Titusville, Pennsylvania

THE WAY
WE LOVE
NOW

"**W**hy, you silly little pussycat," he chuckled warmly, "of course I'll make love to you!"   —*W. R. C. Shedenhelm*
Ventura, California

When the pretty blond slid onto the barstool beside him, Cecil's thin, clammy lips fought wildly against each other for something intelligent to say, finally gave up and instead simply parted, letting fly a tortuous, complicated burp that Cecil hoped would convince her of his raw manliness; and from that tense, charged moment the evening unfolded before him like a badly done piece of origami.

—*Leann Roberts*
Iron Station, North Carolina

Allan, who throughout most of his forty years read only children's stories, found that Mother Goose did not prepare him for his night with Helen, who was illiterate, but worldly.   —*Mike Valcho*
La Mirada, California

"You shall bear many children," he toasted, "and feed them with your ample breasts," and I was sure I'd married the right man.   —*D. Weisman*
Boston, Massachusetts

Little did he know that forty years hence, as he lay on his deathbed, this woman, whose hand he now held, would hold his hand for the last time and confess, one by one, each of the many affairs she had had throughout their marriage which was just about to begin— "I do," he said timidly.

—*Robert Francian*
Anchorage, Alaska

She could not face the thief of her heart, sitting smugly across the table, for he had taken from her the pristine flower of her chastity (on this—their first date) and the grief of her loss was an ever-present lump in the back of her throat that no amount of wailing and gnashing of teeth could remove—no, wait, thank God, it was just a piece of tough brisket, and a finger did the trick.

—*David A. Carter*
Cincinnati, Ohio

He thought he'd never forget the tongue-lashing she braided into the hair on his chest that time he referred to her as the "ball and chain" in that arrogant, cavalier style of his, when he thought she was out of earshot in the kitchen, barefoot and so pregnant he swore he could thump on her belly and hear that hollow echo he always listened for whenever he and the boys would sneak into old man Johnson's melon patch and pick out a couple of casabas as ready for nibbling as her knockers were now, struggling with the buttons on her dickey like two fat kids wrestling in a gunny sack, but this time was even worse; she was already waddling toward him with her eyes spilling angry tears on the barrel of her derringer as she screamed a fingernail-on-the-blackboard screech, "Chick? did you call me a chick?"

—*Nanette Hough*
Mount Vernon, Washington

"Black with one, thanks," she said to Carlo, the joint owner of the local Pizza Parlor Coffee Shop, but he knew by the way she said it, as sure as his moustache was thick and curly, that she wanted him.   *—Kerrie Simpson*
Condell Park, Australia

True, the heat rash was damned unpleasant, but a small price to pay, Marlene thought to herself, for the steamy afternoons with Wally, occasions that had acquainted her, perhaps for the first time, with her own sexuality as well as with the antifungal spray which she now removed from the medicine cabinet.   *—Tom Callison*
Forest City, North Carolina

"Hey, baby!" Cookie LaVamp spat provocatively as she wheeled around on her barstool, jackknifed her legs and hiked her skirt up higher than the markup on a '55 Buick once owned by Elvis, "What makes a man like you so tough and a woman like me so weak?" *—Brian R. McNeill*
Frederick, Maryland

As our lips parted (our last kiss!), I knew then that I would never forget what Christophe and I had shared that summer—no, I shall not forget those winsome, wonderful, wild, wacky weeks—not until the day I become so senile that I am shuffling along a freeway feeder road in robe and slippers, grandchildren trailing after me, shaking their heads sadly and saying, "It's time to put Mee-Maw in a home."   *—Denise Leslie*
Bellaire, Texas

Aristide was nothing more than a wild, impetuous frog-boy, and I a mere slip of a girl, when, with spirits conjoined

for all eternity, we fled hand in hand, more or less, from the nightmarish existence we had known with Madame Monique's European Circus and Side Show, to a life liberated from zany, bumbling clowns and elephants, where, though we knew it not at the time, we were destined to change the course of human evolution and, in the process, repair the crumbling infrastructure of a great American metropolis.   —*Cheryl Aguilar*
Hacienda Heights, California

The still, pensive night sat heavy on the heart of Sylvia, not unlike the last time she had a chili cheese dog with onions, as she gazed longingly across the wide bay, which was as flat as a pepperoni pizza with jalapeños, hoping her true love would return soon with the pistachio chocolate ice cream—this pregnancy was beginning to eat at her nerves.   —*Linda Wensrich*
Sacramento, California

The surgically enhanced blond was a walking advertisement for the craft—perky silicone fluffed D-cup breasts that stood up and shouted, "Take that, cowboy!"; skin so lustrous you'd swear it had just been turtle waxed and buffed; ruby-red collagen-enhanced lips that would have made a Ubangi chieftain break into a cold sweat, and in the greasy glare of the high-tech honky-tonk, I could see she was a disease I had not been vaccinated against.
—*Michael A. Nettleton*
Portland, Oregon

Her Siamese-blue eyes glowed from the murky dark as her Jaguar purred up to my fish bowl of a window, and when I tossed out her chow and she pounced on the pungent bag with a frisky little smile and an arch of her golden eyebrows, I knew this tender blond vittle had just plunged her playful crimson claws deep into my aimlessly circling heart, landing me, gasping, in the drive-through lane of love.

—*Beth Stephenson*
Fort Wayne, Indiana

Even before she opened her eyes that morning, Magda realized her overindulgence in wine at dinner the previous evening had exacted a disgusting price, for she was in a strange bed, the body atop her was kneading her chest, and the breath hot on her neck was that of an old enemy—her host's ill-tempered, partially bald, grossly overweight cat.

—*Mary Anthony*
Grand Rapids, Michigan

She was as lovely as a picnic morning on a Chicago summer's day, and even the flock of flies and gnats that permeated her immediate environment, even the tiny, crystalline beads of sweat that gathered and ran slowly off the tip of her Roman nose, even the ambience of stale, cheap beer, Lifebuoy soap, charcoal starter, and Campbell's Pork and Beans, even all of that was not enough to keep Joe from noticing that Lucrezia was one hell of a woman, and a pretty fair first baseperson, too!

—*Terrence O. Carroll*
San Jose, California

"She'll be back," he thought, "because she knows a quality man when she sees one," and, with a punctuating flick of his wrist he removed the last speck of mildew from his shower grout with her toothbrush.

—*Mark Watson*
Cary, North Carolina

She'd spent most of her life crawling toward that easy street so many stories have described, serving coffee to a well-shaved, tousle-haired, entertaining, share-all husband after a night of sweaty, hurts-so-good, give-me-a-shower-when-it's-over sex, while four perfectly groomed, well-behaved, affectionate offspring frolicked with the ever playful, never-needs-a-bath-or-a-visit-to-the-vet Great Dane.
— *Kim Russell*
Blytheville, Arkansas

Chucky leaned against the jukebox, guzzling the best $1.75 red wine he could buy and thinking of his ex-girlfriend Buffy's tragic death from having the jukebox he was leaning on fall on her, all to the tune of what was their song, "Get Your Tongue out of My Mouth, I'm Trying to Tell You Goodbye."
— *Karra Wolf-Shimabukura*
Manteo, North Carolina

As the wind-whipped branches beat against the house and the rain lashed the windows, she stuffed her meager yet tacky belongings into a shopping bag and prepared to head out into it when the sight of the moon insouciantly riding above it all made her think, "If they can send a man to the moon, why can't they send them all there?"
— *Helen E. Christopher*
Saskatoon, Saskatchewan

It was the night I watched Matilda's tail lights fade into the dust, leaving me like a hubcap spinning along the side of the road after a bootlegger's turn, that I discovered myself, once again, at the self-service island at the gas station of life.
— *Vance Atkins*
Seattle, Washington

When Marie walked through the front door and found her husband Monty locked in a passionate embrace with the housekeeper, the tension was so thick you could have cut it with a knife, not a butter knife, mind you, but one of those big Ginsu jobbies advertised on late-night television for $29.95 that come with a set of steak knives.

—*Kayla H. McAlister*
Calgary, Alberta

MORE
VILE PUNS

"I suggest you stick to painting, Mr. Van Gogh—you sure don't have an ear for music."
—*Lee DiAngelo*
St. Petersburg, Florida

To most people it seemed to be a group of salamanders partying 'til they puked, but to Eustace it was nothing less than a newt gang-retch.
—*Rev. William F. Charles*
Cassopolis, Michigan

Looking all around at the shattered and collapsed buildings, cracked streets and broken water mains in his Southern California hometown, Jason shook his head and said, "The San Andreas couldn't have done this!" but he had always been generous to a fault.
—*John L. Ashman*
Houston, Texas

"This book," sneered Spooner, as he flung the volume down on an end table and, in so doing, smashed a small octopus, "really whacks a polyp."
—*David Krassner*
Newport Beach, California

Because the death of her Saint Bernard had buried Heide under an emotional avalanche, it was only holy, oily Ole O'Leahy who, as spiritual guide to the Mazola

Yodeling Team, had the power to help her climb out of her valley of despair and challenge the slopes of adversity with a song on her lips by reminding her that the Lord alps those who alp themselves.   —*Dallas Brozik*
Huntington, West Virginia

On his first day on the job as a butcher, Frank backed into the meat grinder and, before he knew it, he had gotten a little behind in his orders.   —*Jeff Ottney*
Titusville, Pennsylvania

It retrospect, it probably wasn't the best idea to deliver a complimentary 825-pound vat of grits to the Song of the South Choir Festival, thought Alton Harley Scruggs III, owner of the Spartanburg, South Carolina–based True Grits diner chain, especially after surveying the havoc that ensued when the balsa wood bargain he'd bought for $55.17 at Pat's Discount Vats failed to contain its edible cargo, spewing it onto the stage like Prestone from a busted radiator; yet, happily, the contest went on anyway, and everyone ended up singing in hominy.
—*Brian D. Smith*
New Whiteland, Indiana

The episode started when Thackeray, the pet cat of the library, ate one of the largest books, causing him to get a severe case of main tome poisoning. —*Richard W. O'Bryan*
Perrysburg, Ohio

"I can swim faster than you can, and I'm much more maneuverable," said the paramecium superciliously to the amoeba.   —*Michael J. Saxton*
Riverside, California

Gideon unwisely decided to use as entrée the remainder of yesterday's breakfast oatmeal, flambéed with two hundred-proof rum, for, as he ignited the dish the resultant conflagration caused him to gush, "There's no fuel like an old gruel!"

—*C. A. Hall*
Holton, Indiana

I wanted to begin my State of the Union address to the American people with "render unto Caesar" but my writers hollered, "That'll just put folks in mind of the killing Hillary made on pork bellies," so instead I spoke of my wife's staunch moral fiber and ended the oratory with "Like Caesar's wife, she is above reproach"—I reckon that's why it's known as the "righting Rodham" text.

—*Marlene May*
Vancouver, British Columbia

Clad in a crisp, white linen suit, Witherspoon Pasha, the Cairo police's director of criminal investigations, ignoring the heat and noise of the dingy native cafe, drew upon his water pipe, turned to his faithful assistant, Ibrahim Pasha, and remarked, "Is it not strange that I, who am accustomed to the company of the most beautiful and high-born ladies in Cairo, should be spending this evening with a hookah?"

—*Howard Cooper*
Chevy Chase, Maryland

Deep in the Dakota badlands Sandy Park and a crack crew of dinosaur diggers unloaded their pack animals near a paleontological paradise of finely fossilized prehistoric predators and while they searched for a name for this Mesozoic mausoleum suddenly Sandy's four-legged beast of burden lost its lunch on Sandy's genuine L.L. Bean

Camp Mocs, and Professor Rex Tyrone asked, "Your ass sick, Park?"
—John L. Ashman
Houston, Texas

After he moved into the small Maine hamlet that dark winter, the wealthy stranger swiftly rented both the cursed Bates Motel and the House on Haunted Hill, making him, the townsfolk all whispered, the lessor of two evils.
—Robert L. Bryant, Jr.
Columbia, South Carolina

I took one look in the mirror on the wall, saw the sneezy red-eyed look of pain on my face instead of my normally handsome prince-like features, and knew my days as a huntsman were over, since an allergy to wicked Queen Anne's lace and an accidental shot through my snow white buns had landed me in the emergency room with a grumpy lady doc who left me blushing and bashful when she gave me a shot in the rear that made me dopey and sleepy but happy that the forest animals didn't have to worry about me anymore.
—Allison Beilue Thompson
Edmond, Oklahoma

These are the times that try men's soles, and so it went with the shoe salesman, wizened face like leather, as he pounded the pavement day after day, peddling his products, digging in his heels to stem the slide in a business that had suffered from unethical businessmen, heels really, whose loafing and pumping up of their own egos had resulted in foot-dragging, particularly when the signs of the oncoming recession would require everyone to pull himself up by his own bootstraps.
—Stephen E. Yandell
Peabody, Massachusetts

As a highly competent computer programmer in her own right, Barbara enjoyed her professional (and non-professional) relationship with Fred (known as Professor by the upper echelon of the syndicate, who appreciated his computer skills and financial wizardry, and Freddy the Nerd by those who didn't), and so she resented the crime reporter of the Valley *Gazette*'s always referring to her as a hood ornament.
                                          —*Richard Patching*
                                          Calgary, Alberta

Cloistered in an ancient monastery high in the French Alps, theoretical economist Jacques Cannou struggled to complete his comprehensive model of society's reaction to panhandlers, totally unaware that his model was to become the watchword of the Great Depression— "Brother Cannou's Paradigm."   —*Gordon K. Anderson*
                                          Crestline, California

"Wouldn't let me join in any reindeer games, eh?" thought a bitter Rudolph, his red nose glowing angrily in the dense fog, as he slipped from the bell-studded harness and watched eight of his tormentors, a sleigh full of toys, and St. Nicholas, too, smash into the mountain slope.

—*Cora Williams Weisenberger*
Richton Park, Illinois

"I don't think we're in Kansas anymore, Toto," whispered Dorothy as she watched the happy little people singing and dancing around them, "these Munchkins think I killed the Wicked Witch of the East, and besides, they just don't act like Republicans." —*John L. Ashman*
Houston, Texas

The bullet had entered the right frontal lobe of the brain and exited through the back of the cerebellum before it grazed a pink marshmallow chick and lodged in the chocolate-coated peanut-butter creme egg, but it was the shiny bits of dentin and enamel crunching beneath my heel that revealed the stark and brutal truth—the Tooth Fairy had smoked the Easter Bunny. —*Ann Brownell*
Portland, Oregon

Daphne ran swiftly across the windswept moor scarcely noticing its heather perfume, down to the rocky cliff where she paused momentarily atop the jagged precipice, looked down at the waves crashing far below, and wished that she had been born anything other than a lemming.
—*Daniel R. Little*
Huntsville, Alabama

Goody Twoshoes sat in the little house on the hill with Freddy Fly and Susie Spider and Harriet Hornet, cursing whatever blackhearted divvil it was that used the last pages of the old Sears and Roebuck catalog, leaving her only the stiff, nonabsorbent covers.
—*Carl Pavel*
Chicago, Illinois

Six-year-old Lindy Lou, tears slipping from brimming eyes wider than cornflower-blue Fiestaware saucers to plaster her flaxen curls against the sides of her tiny heart-shaped face, shrunk even further into the engulfingly plush movie seat away from the onscreen horror of Bambi's mother roasting to agonizing death in the forest fire like a marshmallow fallen from a S'More, and with wounded innocence bleeding from every pore of her being, choked out a hiccupy sob not unlike a Ford engine trying to turn over a January morning in Calgary, "Oh, Mommy, what a lousy waste of venison!"
—*Robin B. Shore*
Belmont, Massachusetts

Stunned at first by the spectacle of his mother's smoldering remains, Bambi grieved for a moment, then, remembering the code of the wild, philosophized, "Better her than me!"
—*Ricky Horton*
Asotin, Washington

This story is of Sparky, the heroic Doberman who was my favorite pet, not only because he brought me the paper and my slippers every morning, but because he saved my life the time I got stranded in the mountains for a week by becoming a nice warm pillow for the first four nights and dinners that tasted something like chicken for the final three.

—*Susan Kanda*
Sunnyvale, California

When the shiny new engine refused to help the little train carry its jolly load over the mountain, G.I. Joe blew off its wheels with his bazooka, Teenage Mutant Ninja Turtles turned the engineer into a shapeless sack of bone fragments, and then a gang of Transformers salvaged parts from the smoking hulk which they reassembled into shiny new toy assault weapons for all the good little boys and girls who lived on the other side of the mountain.

—*Johnny Davis*
Valdosta, Georgia

It was a big, brave, blue, and beautiful morning, Happy Harry Hedgehog decided, as he prepared to waddle purposefully, slowly, and fatefully across the four lanes of the busy interstate. (From *A Child's Garden of Roadkill*)

—*Terrence O. Carroll*
San Jose, California

Little Gustifer loved to eat Gummi Worms, chewing and chewing them or putting them into his mouth and drawing them out his nose while singing, "The worms crawl in; the worms crawl out/the worms play pinochle in your snout!" little realizing that very soon he would

be run over by a car and become food for worms himself.
—*Marina True*
Berkeley, California

Reputedly nimble and quick but with "White men can't jump" ringing in his ears, Jack jumped and tripped over the candlestick and cracked his left patella in almost as many places as Humpty Dumpty's shell, but not quite.
—*John L. Ashman*
Houston, Texas

Once upon a time, there was a boy named Ricky, who liked to go on camping trips just like *this* camping trip, and he learned all about what to do if you get lost in the woods, and it's a good thing Ricky knew all the important stuff I'm going to teach you because, sure enough, Ricky got lost—but he didn't panic, no sirree, he just sat right down and hugged a tree and, you know what?—when they found his skeleton three years later he was still hugging that tree.
—*Cynthia Conyers*
Warner Springs, California

I was born penniless; my diapers had no pockets.
—*David Slotkoff*
New York, New York

Closing the door behind her, Little Red Riding Hood strode over to the couch, removed her little red riding hood, dropped her little red riding crop, kicked off her little red leather riding boots, knocked back a triple scotch, took two puffs from a cigarette, looked up at the ceiling, and exclaimed aloud, "Bugger this! only three cus-

tomers this week—I wonder if business is better over at Grannie's?"
—*Alexander J. Edmonds*
Blackburn, Australia

Alice lay dreamily under the tree as her sister's dry little voice buzzed on like a distant cicada through the interminable history lesson, until in her depression she began again to think of large, furry *muscular* white rabbits, and her hand crept on a familiar journey beneath her skirt.
—*Richard Raymond III*
Roanoke, Virginia

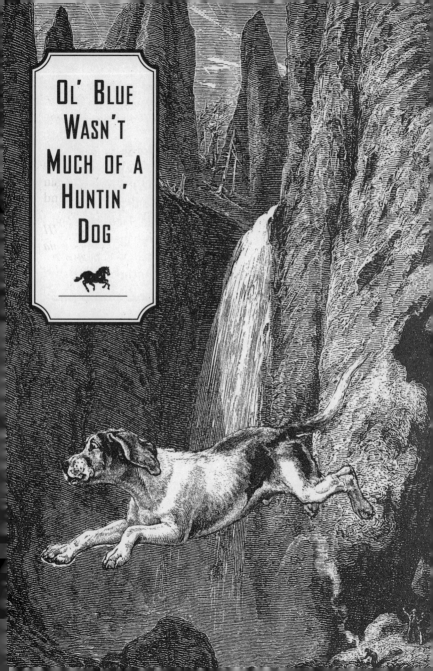

Ol' Blue Wasn't Much of a Huntin' Dog

FROM *Bride of Dark and Stormy* (1988)

Ordinary men, broken and ravaged by the scouring prairie winds, would have looked through sand-stung eyes at the bleak sea of dry grass across the Nebraska landscape and given up, and Ned Bimpler was one of these men.

—*Wanda E. Seamster*
Anchorage, Alaska

Ol' Blue wasn't much of a huntin' dog—a gun-shy, bob-tailed, floppy-eared varmint who smelled like a zoo and shed his hair in crusty clumps—but when the grandkids came to call he'd lie on the floor and roughhouse with little Clement and lick the baby's cheek, and he'd rip the throat out of anybody who carried a briefcase.

—*Robert Y. Kline*
Roseville, Minnesota

One evening, after a particularly large serving of Granny Mae's barbecued baked beans, Feral Timsley apprehensively hiked up his boxer shorts and gazed out the crescent-shaped cutout in the musty old outhouse, thinking it was an exciting thing to be airborne and headed for the unknown, but there was no more paper.

—*Lean Roberts*
Iron Station, North Carolina

On that dusty day when the Wild Thing Diner surrendered its access road to the new Route 9 interchange, Gus, the cook, and Frizie, the waitress, got it on across the cigarette-scarred top of table 8, while the spoon and fork dials on the grease-splattered wall clock served up the noonday special—and afterwards they toasted to better times and vowed to squeeze the juice out of life and keep their smiles sunny-side up, while Ramos, the dishwasher, filled his jittery vein to the brim with a rich Colombian brew.
    —*Janet Paszkowski*
    Alpharetta, Georgia

With soft golden hair like sunshine spun into flowing silk, delicate hands seemingly created expressly to caress tender spring blossoms, cheeks so rosy and unblemished that they might have been taken intact from a porcelain doll, and eyes so clearly blue that they stole nature's own color from the sky above, Bubba Hagerfield had long ago learned to expect snide remarks from the other mechanics at Charlie Odum's Highway 47 (Business) Auto Repair Shop.
    —*Ed Gibbon*
    Houston, Texas

As she languished on the sweet smelling straw in the bed of his rusted 1952 Chevrolet pickup, the mid-afternoon sun warming her naked pink flesh, Cynthia suddenly shuddered, her vacant eyes narrowed to slits, and it became abruptly clear to her at that moment that Farmer Ron had lied—she *was* just like all the other pigs . . .
    —*Robert A. Arnold*
    Portage, Michigan

She was all alone in the freshly bushhogged cowfield while the cattle inched ever closer as they chewed their regurgitated cud in almost rhythmic fashion, with the pungent aroma of the cow manure that oozed between her supple toes wafting up to her enormously large nostrils, all the while her blue eyes darting to the left and right, searching for an opening in the closing circle of cattle, and somewhere, off in the distance, a dog barked.

—*Lisa Joy Bowlin*
Franklin, Ohio

"Manifest Destiny!" he cried raggedly as he uncovered his new bride's nubile body, so like the new land which he longed to conquer—wild, lovely, and free, yet pure and unspoiled, and soon to be changed forever by the thrust of his western expansion.

—*Nancy Vitavec*
Chico, California

A bunch of the boys were whoopin' it up down at the Cogito Ergo Sum Saloon, when in through the louvered swinging doors waltzes Kid Camus wearin' a lean, mean prove-it-to-me-that-you-exist kind of look.

—*Steven Schaubel*
Minneapolis, Minnesota

"Yeah, they called him Rocky Stagecoach 'cause that's where he was born . . . on the bumpy trail between Conception and Contusion."

—*Rix Quinn*
Fort Worth, Texas

The column halted at the Little Puddle River, while "New Hampshire Dick" Baltenschwaltz, our scout, splashed across it to converse with the Indian warrior on the other side, then returning from his palaver he spat into the river and drawled, "Waal, Lootenant, that thar jasper

'cross the river is either the son of old Turkey-Inconvenienced-the-Gopher and means to have our hair if we cross this yar crick, *or* he's a albino Bulgarian transvestite come west to sell tin roofing and whalebone corsets to the Injuns: ain't him or me too good talkin' with our hands, so just take yer pick."
—*Robert D. Norris, Jr.*
Tulsa, Oklahoma

Bloodthirsty, cunning, cruel—Running Fox, war chief of the Cheyenne, was all those things, but he also rode the cutting edge of tribal fashion; and so it was that, after his braves massacred the wagon load of immigrants from Yugoslavia and Bangkok and took their scalps in the spring of 1861, he became the first Indian to wear a Croat and Thai.
—*Robert L. Bryant, Jr.*
Columbia, South Carolina

"Nope—that ain't no Injun village, ma'am," explained old Jed patiently as he aimed a yellow stream of tobacco juice at a low flying turkey buzzard, "that there's Laramie—the exterminators are tenting for varmints."
—*John L. Ashman*
Houston, Texas

PLAIN
BROWN
WRAPPERS

FROM *Bride of Dark and Stormy* (1988)

As she lay there sleeping next to me, one voice inside my head kept saying, "Relax . . . you're not the first doctor who's ever slept with one of his patients," but another kept reminding me, "Howard, you're a veterinarian." —*Dick Wilson*
Orlando, Florida

She named her parakeet Onan, for he spilled his seed upon the ground. —*Kristen Kingsbury Henshaw*
Wakefield, Massachusetts

"Holmes!" I ejaculated, instantly cluing the attentive reader that either this was yet another parody of the famed Baker Street duo, or else that the novel's obligatory sex scene had prematurely climaxed. —*Mark Bernstein*
Yellow Springs, Ohio

"I wanted a seven but I got a three, which means I crapped out," Saul whined to his young wife, who sighed and became lost once again in the tall croupier's mesmerizing cant: "Time to play the field, come bets, horn bets, who wants a hard eight coming out?" —*Johnny Davis*
Valdosta, Georgia

Peering into the hen house with lecherous eyes, Spanky stuffed the rubber gloves back into his unzipped pants—it would be more thrilling to choke the chicken barehanded.

—*Matthew Engelke*
Alta Loma, California

As Hapless, the young apprentice Wizard of Blockhead, cradled the trembling body of the beauteous Lady Broadbum, whose body he had just delivered from its demonic possession, he sensed that events of even greater import were about to transpire: the room had suddenly grown hot and his pants hurt.

—*Susan Lea Farrell*
Prescott, Arizona

As two bodies lost in purple passion lay entwined on the golden sandy shore in the violet twilight of a summer's eve, the lighthouse beam probed the dark night, a foghorn's melancholy tone penetrated the moist enveloping darkness, the pounding surf surged, retreated and thrust again and again with rhythmic relentless determination, the wild fingers of water plunged into the rocky clefts lined with soft moist squirting anemones, resilient yet yielding; and cobbles rolled in the lapping wavelets with ecstatic abandon, the heaving lovers were engulfed with a climactic tidal bore of rapture as their juices of passion mingled primevally with the warm salty sea—but in the end it was just gritty.

—*Adriana Karwick Larkin*
Half Moon Bay, California

"The thrust of all this," spewed the erect and turgid prosecutor, "is that this film is pornographic," but the judge didn't swallow it, leaving the D.A. to bemoan the

fact that His Honor was not abreast of current penal statutes.
—*Mark Watson*
Cary, North Carolina

It was larger than she thought it would be, and she stared in horror as the oblong, fleshy object, foamy white substance escaping from one end, loomed towards her, and she squealed in mock terror, "No matter what you try to make me do, I will not put that *thing* in my mouth . . . even if Twinkies are an American tradition."
—*Rachael Osborn*
Albuquerque, New Mexico

"Ah, Juliet," murmured the young Montague, "if thou refrainest not from shrieking 'F***! C***! S***! C*********!' and the like, in the midst of our conjugal conditioning, I fear that ours will be a star-crossed love."
—*Richard Raymond III*
Roanoke, Virginia

Upon explaining foreplay to her young, unexperienced daughter/bride-to-be, the mother remarked, "Your father likes to bark like a dog, foam at the mouth, urinate on the bed, and rub up and down against my leg . . . however, you should be aware that not all men are as romantic as your dad."
—*Peter Vrana, Jr.*
Sunnyvale, California

It had been a sumptuous wedding night, and after experiencing the Supreme Moment in the arms of his willing bride, he remembered his youthful travails as a pupil of Brother Odo, the tedium of Latin lessons and Odo's insistence on the short, oft-repeated Latin prayers, and he

thought, Brother, your pious ejaculations ain't got nothing
on this.
—*Anne Butzen*
Chicago, Illinois

The beautiful and seductive Lila Adams took the prof-
fered book, glanced at the title, *A Charlie Brown's
Christmas*, slammed it back into his midsection, and
stormed, cursing, from the room, leaving a stunned, and
very confused, Richard Tyler, who was positive she had
begged to see his "Peanuts."
—*F. James Welch*
Brockport, New York

Tiffany trembled when he touched her hand—hairs
leapt up like meerkats on sentry duty all along her body,
and she felt a vacuum suck between them as blood
dumped into her pelvis, pounding, pulsing, pushing mois-
ture into her panties; sweat became her second skin, slipping down between her breasts and buttocks, gluing her
thighs together, puddling in her pumps.

—*Cindy Robinson*
Knoxville, Tennessee

Commander Denise Creighton, looking forward to
some support in her job as chief U.S. medical officer on the
navy base in Gortanola, walked past the banana trees to
the aircraft and introduced herself to Lieutenant Davis,
whose eyes locked hers in a vise-like grip, probing and
breaching all of her defenses and sending her brain into a
dizzying spiral as he pulled her limp and willing body to
his own, then together they fell quivering and heaving to
the sizzling tarmac, she his and he hers, their clothes mere
blades of grass in the hurricane of their passion, as she

thought, "Just like all the others—he never even bothered
to salute!"
—*Jeff Laufle*
Seattle, Washington

Wilmer relived the deliciousness of clipping off
Hollywood Barbie's long platinum hair to a rough stubble,
popping off her head and gulping it down to join Malibu
Barbie's and the others neatly lined up in his lower colon,
then grunted ecstatically as the exquisitely bristly doll
heads began their return journey to the outside world.
—*Cynthia Conyers*
Warner Springs, California

The storm raged and the wind shrieked and the sea
roared and the sky twitched and the masts creaked and the
planks groaned and the aft rose and the stern sank and her
breasts heaved and his loins stirred, and the question
remained only whether his seed or his lunch would first
burst into the steaming darkness.
—*David Hirsch*
Seattle, Washington

"Call me Irresponsible," she wailed as she deliberately,
but carelessly, threw the condom overboard, grazing the
rail before it penetrated the warm waters of the Pacific;
and, in the ensuing silence (quiet only for the sporadic
spouting of indigenous sperm whales), the boat gently
rocked back and forth, back and forth, while she lay on the
deck and gazed pregnantly at the great white sail flutter-
ing in the moonlight above her and her lover, Dick Moby.
—*P. J. Carey*
Germantown, Maryland

George felt strangely disassociated as cool fingertips
traced the line of his crisp brown body hair down into his

bulging Italian-cut briefs—making love was always fun
. . . even now when he was alone, he considered, as the
Velcro gave way. —*Heather Alexandra Pierce*
Kent, Washington

It was only when, with a searing pain, her own tropic of
Capricorn was deforested that Veronica comprehended her
unfortunate plight: the inexpensive new Henry Miller edi-
tion she had begun to grind between her quivering thighs
was not signature bound, as she well knew, nor even
perfect-bound, as she'd assumed, but—ah, cruel irony!—
was saddle-stitched with Bostich number twos.

—*Jon Jefferson*
Knoxville, Tennessee

Feeling a bit out of sorts from having barely survived an
extremely painful shaving experience, I stepped out of the
steamy bathroom wearing Frederick's Of Hollywood silky
blue pajama bottoms and so many tattered pieces of toilet
paper stuck to my face it looked like I'd fallen headfirst
into a cactus garden because the Old Lady had used my
razor on her legs and, God help me, her armpits; and
walked into the cheerless bedroom that was glaringly lit by
a dusty ceiling fixture that shone like a beacon and spot-
lighted her nude body sprawled in the center of our dilap-
idated double bed where she resembled a collapsed
dumpling with breasts sliding off into obscurity and coming to rest on either side of her body, much like a couple
of elbow macaronis without the cheese, and I thought, this
can't be the Sweet Little Thing who raised my hormones
to uncontrollable levels twenty years ago, and I said,
"Gertrude, put your teeth in, you look just like your
mother." —*Barbara Sharik Vail*
Jones, Louisiana

As Warp
Speed
Rattled
the Bridge

FROM *It Was a Dark and Stormy Night* (1984)

The surface of the strange, forbidden planet was roughly textured and green, much like cottage cheese gets way after the date on the lid says it is all right to buy it.

—*Scott Davis Jones*
Sausalito, California

It was a black-backdropped set with pinpoints of white light and a teal wardroom; the technobabble fell in torrents—except at occasional intervals, when it was checked by a stentorian "Make it so!" (for it is on the *Enterprise* that our bad acting lies), as warp speed rattled the bridge and fiercely agitated both the on-screen display and Commander Riker's clinch with the scantily-clad alien, and Data struggled with his script. —*Robert S. Kendall*
Shorewood, Illinois

Those alarm things that make a real loud honking kind of noise were going off as Captain James Hurley stared at the screen that showed him the stuff that was outside in space while he sat in the chair that the captain sits in, and slowly reached for the control panel for the thing that makes the ship go real fast. —*Tom Butler*
Tallahassee, Florida

The time machine had worked perfectly, landing Professor Thwaitcastle gently on Plymouth Rock just as the Mayflower appeared on the horizon, but unfortunately there were several other time machines and their occupants already there waiting to observe this, the first successful case of time travel.   —*David K. Crandall*
                                               Sherman Oaks, California

"Where in the hell is Ginger?" screamed her partner astaireically, remembering with anguish the lie she had lain on Punctuality's doorstep—she had promised to early-bird her arrival—and already stomping on eggshells because he wasn't about to take this layer of lies lying down, knowing the truth—that they were neither the real Fred nor the real Ginger, being instead duplicitous doppelgangers who had been sent from Saturn to steal the secret of dancing on ceilings.   —*Carlos W. Colon*
                                                   Shreveport, Louisiana

Lamona Desponder from the multoid planet Oberslatzburg d'Freug near the Circle of Hardley and a lustrum lifemaster of Inter-Galactic KuFu Bridge smiled knowingly, revealing a row of small cherry-red tusks, when Zozo Bonerette, a Lyborian Eyesore from the Nasalton Plexstar and her favorite duplicate partner, bid four zils, obviating the need for Lamona to play her only living trump card, the two of centipedes.   —*Charlie Mattson*
                                                     Columbus, Ohio

The ghostly green light of the radar screen reflected dully off the beads of cold perspiration which had suddenly appeared on Sergeant Ted Corman's face as he tracked the mysterious blips which changed directions far

too rapidly, and he wondered if and how this would ultimately tie in with the radio frequency disturbances, the dramatic increase in whale beachings, and the ham-and-guacamole sandwiches that were inexplicably turning up in lunch pails all over the world.　　　—*Robert Phillips*
Lakeland, Florida

Before drifting back to sleep, Fran replayed the event in her head (which was so fresh she could still see Jimmy's long lost Frisbee on the roof of her house), and as Harvey's loud snores drowned out the sound of her pounding heart, she was certain that, not only had she just been beamed aboard an alien spacecraft, but that she had been right about the Morrisons keeping a goat on their patio.

—*F. Shaw-Brabazon*
Hensonville, New York

It was early morning in Antarctica, February 2, 1999, and Professor Bradbury was working feverishly to ready his experiment—an enormous groundhog-shaped weather balloon—in the desperate hope that Ozone Oscar, to be sent aloft to peep through the widening hole in the atmosphere, would not see his shadow, and thus would end what had been a long and difficult nuclear winter.

—*Mary Leah Christmas*
Dover, Delaware

In retrospect, we decided that the nuclear winter was not so bad, but that we had not really enjoyed the brief but intense nuclear summer that had preceded it.

—*Richard Patching*
Calgary, Alberta

"No one could have predicted a solar storm," thought Danko as his starship pulled 14.3566 gravities in its struggle to escape the Tau Ceti gravity well, "but I really wasn't planning on leaving our observation station so soon, and it's just damn hard to get a crew to do anything when they're pinned against the bulkheads unable to move for a week at a time," and he yelled into the intercom, "Patton, you are going to clean up the mess you've made by pumping coffee into these people for the last six Earth-standard days!"
—*Jeff Laufle*
Seattle, Washington

After collecting samples of the light spectrum reflected from the lunar surface, the alien ship shot off toward the local sun, swinging through its powerful gravity well to increase the craft's velocity for the return trip to the distant home world of Sirius VII, as the crew listened to an ever-diminishing radio signal from the surface of the blue planet: " . . . or would you rather swing on a star, and take a moonbeam home in a jar?"
—*David K. Crandall*
Sherman Oaks, California

CELEBRATING
DIVERSITY

FROM *It Was a Dark and Stormy Night* (1984)

He was a Portuguese who had never fished and she was a Chinese who couldn't cook rice; he had enough hair on his chest to make a coat for a very small Hungarian and the way she kissed it made him wonder why.

—*Don Austin*
Vancouver, British Columbia

Try as he might, Guido Smith could not get into the spirit of Oktoberfest this year; his laissez-faire cum mañana attitude made him want to say sayonara to the whole shebang.
—*Marc Roberge*
Santa Rosa, California

Mrs. Nakazawa entered the room, honoring me with the formal Japanese "bobbing for apples" bow as Mr. Nakazawa pointed a playing card out the window at the unusual black bird and shouted "Rook! Rook!" and I realized at that moment that we were all different yet the same—the bird black, myself white, the Nakazawas Japanese.
—*Maren Hoven*
St. Paul, Minnesota

"Tu manges la glace et dit merde," she hissed vehemently over the order of dim sum alfredo, ignoring

Torvald's keening, poignant rendition of "Bei Mir Bist Du
Schon."
—*Jane Dioguardi Plantz*
Meriden, Connecticut

A dozen flies, wheeling and volplaning in the heavy
night air redolent with the scent of jasmine, traces of wood
smoke from the Malay village, and an occasional acrid
whiff from the elephant pens across the river, would some-
times land on the face and lips of the beautiful, sleeping
servant girl lost in dreams of her forthcoming marriage to
Ranjit Singh, unaware that the microbes on their sticky
feet would cause her excruciating death of cholera on
the night before her marriage, leaving Ranjit Singh to consider his own suicide.
—*Robert G. Worman*
Seminole, Florida

The Spanish moss hung low on the Canadian oak as the
German band played "Blue Danube," and Chinese fire-
works burst in a cascade of Icelandic blues and Russian
reds while we ate Swiss cheese and Italian sausage on
French bread to celebrate the Fourth of July.
—*Janet L. Clark*
Boca Raton, Florida

"Oh yes, yes, yes," moaned Lenore, responding to the
deep, soulful kisses that quickly brought her to full arousal
from her gentle slumber, only to be unpleasantly surprised
to find it was not Momar, the Lebanese gigolo who flitted
in and out of her life whose tongue was halfway down her
throat, but Bingo, her lusty chimpanzee with the gable-
like ears— "Oh no, no, no, well, maybe."
—*Blair Thurman*
Reston, Virginia

Flipper glidded effortlessly through the pale blue Florida water, the young Scandinavian girl, Ilga, at his side, while the marine biologists stood on the shore near by, marveling at this wonder of nature—this dolphin with an extra Finn.
—*Bill Robinson*
Canal Fulton, Ohio

"Eat lead, you scumbag," Guido muttered silently to himself as he placed the Frutti di Mare al Fredo before the distended belly of Alfonse "the Gutter" Gutermo, knowing that the miniscule dose of lead sulfate would not be detected, but would, after years of weekly ingestion, result in some pretty dreadful symptoms.
—*Allen L. Parsley*
Berkeley, California

The shot cried out in the cool, clear, crisp night air, piercing the skull of Amhad Aba Billy Bob Raghib, Asian terrorist, 7-11 employee of the month, and master of the accordion, causing an unstoppable chain of events that included the rebirth of the communist empire, Phil Donahue's getting a Mohawk, and Dan Quayle's becoming pope, but that's not important to our story.
—*Christopher Nekolny*
Woodridge, Illinois

Compulsively working the Western Pacific Rim Smorgasbord from north to south, Chester, vice president of the Gourmet Club, savored heaping plates of Vladivostok herring, Korean kimchee, Taiwanese lo mein, and Thaipai chicken with a Singapore Sling to wash it all down; then he gave new meaning to "spilling one's guts" when a diet-crazed former member knifed open his midriff,

regrettably before Chester's favorite pineapple Jakarta flambé had been set out for dessert.   —*Jim Cuddy*
East Syracuse, New York

My personal odyssey began quite abruptly as I was blasted bolt upright shortly before dawn by the trumpeting of a French hornist amid the Spanish moss outside my window; so, wide awake, I donned my Italian suit, splashed on some English Leather, and paused to write a check; then, realizing I was hungry, I stepped through the Dutch doors into the kitchen to feast on Belgian waffles washed down with Swiss Miss and a drop of Scotch, before whistling for my Irish wolfhound to join me in my German roadster as I went rushing off to look for America.

—*Carolyn Clark*
Brooklyn, New York

"Awww!" exclaimed Reggie, though he was really thinking, "What a stupid waste of 38 quackeroons and sixpence!" as his new Digby Brothers CD slipped from his hand and rolled down the gutter into the rat-infested sewer of Wapsutta, his hometown, capital city of the Republic of Banguto, "Precious Jewel of the Orient."

—*Dave Adcock*
Austin, Texas

He was a dark and stormy Irishman, his face was as porous and bushy as a peat bog, his nose as bulbous as a potato, laced with red and blue veins as gaudy as the British flag he abhorred, and when he bared his stubby broken teeth like wind-lashed fence posts, his anger was both at his English motherland and mother, and at the

"ould sod," by which he meant not his fatherland but his
father.   —*Patricia Spaeth*
                                          Port Townsend, Washington

The Winthropes had eagerly anticipated a fulfilling culi-
nary ensemble of *pâté au fois gras*, *jambon de bernaise avec les
truffles*, *poulet dijon*, and *sorbet*—not at all the collard greens,
ribs, chitlins, fried sweetbreads, and slice o' melon on de
side smorgasbord which their newly appointed cook,
Roberta Robinson, now set before them.
                                          —*Jim "Quasimofo" Sheppeck*
                                                 Irvine, California

Sadiq ali Bronelowski tended his peanuts and dreamed
that one day he would change his name and become president.   —*Graham Reader*
                                               Calgary, Alberta

LYTTONY
III

Andre, a simple peasant, had only one thing on his mind as he crept along the east wall: "Andre creep . . . Andre creep . . . Andre creep."   —*David Allen Janzen*
Sacramento, California

"Why, you silly little fool," the king snickered, "what makes you think you're qualified to be the court jester?"
—*W. R. C. Shedenhelm*
Ventura, California

Todd, who was a light sleeper and rarely remembered his dreams of his grandmother, the burnt-out stripper whose thighs had long ago sabotaged her chances at stardom and relegated her career to community theater mediocrity, and whose late-night rendezvous with all manner of Tom, Dick, and Harry had no doubt contributed to Todd's tendency toward light sleep and seldom remembered dreams, like the one just ending, awoke.
—*John R. Ellingson*
Newport Beach, California

This is the story, dear reader, of how brave little Barney Heston traveled back through history in Ol' Lucy, his

uncle's time machine, and warned young Benito Mussolini not to buy a ticket on the *Titanic*. —*Daniel R. Little*
Huntsville, Alabama

As her vnrvly son's escaped pet serpent vndvlated langvidly across the cervlean blve tiles, Mater (vtterly vnnerved, her vvvla fairly qvivering with fear in the back of her throat) sqvealed, "Clavdivs, Clavdivs, yov'd better shvt that vgly viper back vp in its cage right this minvte, before yovr Pater gets home from the forvm!"
—*Sharon Bliss Brown*
San Mateo, California

With brute, unthinking motions, Herr Beethoven groped across the piano top with his clumsy left hand like a blinded, stupefied beast, toward the false confidence of his nearly drained beer stein, even as the fingers of his right hand fumbled aimlessly over the keyboard, stumbling toward the by-now familiar broken C-sharp minor triads in the second inversion, belching uncouthly while barking gruffly at Katrina, the terrified new housekeeper, "Have you started the turnips yet? I like 'em real good and mushy!" —*Rich Clancey*
Brookline, Massachusetts

"Bitch!" she screamed, "hellcat!" as Fifi, then Fluffy, minced haughtily past the pet food that she had spent the whole morning trying, with one of those can openers that just skates all over the lid instead of piercing it and missing her session with Raoul, to open. —*Anne Emery*
Halifax, Nova Scotia

The summer sun shone through the lace curtains purchased by Theodora's great grandmother, the crazy one, in

1846 from a Parisian woman exiled from her country because of sympathies for the ruling class and a habit of opening her mouth at inopportune moments, and faded the carpet. —*Diana Bridgforth*
Rochester, Minnesota

For a long time I would lie awake, the velvet darkness closing its thick fist like a cloying chocolate that one recalls half eating in the kitchen of my aunt's cottage in Combray, the effluvious smell of her clove tea rolling through my nostrils, a darkness deeper yet then the confessional at the Church of St. Hilaire, whose effulgent candlelight reflects on the oily surface of the oaken reredos, and whose steeple can be seen as far as Balbec, afraid of the deep bass notes of thunder penetrating in desultory rhythm the even hiss of the persistent rainfall, whose sound would inevitably bring me back to the beach at Balbec and my beloved Albertine, for whom the distant pounding seemed to me to be the muffled drum of a dirge to one whose moribund love was apprehended too late. —*Robert Phillips*
Lakeland, Florida

"Rats," exclaimed Portentia, portentously aloud to no one, in tragically belated response to the question "Name two things that scare you" asked of her once by David, who not only was no longer in the room but had in fact long ago left her for another woman, "and mice." —*Richard E. Schmidle*
Rochester, New York

"You can go kiss yourself," Alexis Tick, whose gutter mouth offended me and my fellow teenagers because we don't believe in using that kind of language, but whom we

never suspected of being connected to the recent serial killings because in our permissive society we bury our heads in the sand and tell ourselves that kids (even those who use such language) are basically good when in real life they're all evil, said. —*Bill Bystricky*
Sunnyvale, California

I knew it was going to be one of those days when Mum, the queen, strode into my apartment without knocking, scaring the unclad Camille nearly out of her gorgeous gourd, and broke over the royal knee in furious contempt my best Lil' Blue boomerang. —*Gayle Rogers Lockwood*
Salem, Oregon

When I entered the posh office, Terrance Turnbull III rose from behind his large antique teak desk, a highly polished piece of furniture with intricate dovetailing and beautifully mortised joints that had a long, honorable history in the firm from the time it had been "liberated" by an ever-so-great grandfather from a British garrison in New York City during the Revolutionary War and then smuggled to Albany and hidden in a barn belonging to a Mary Thatcher, a noble and patriotic lady whose husband beat her at the least provocation when he was in his cups, and offered his hand in greeting. —*Creston Munger*
Union Springs, New York

Having caught her lover in the arms of another, Chas had unwittingly (but effectively) driven a stake into Amanda's heart, which was bad enough, but the boy scout next door had tried to tether a tent to it, and it bucked and jerked in the wind. —*David A. Carter*
Cincinnati, Ohio

It was a hot and sunny day that blazed down on the meadow, making the grass shine as bright as the reflection off the patent leather shoes of a Catholic schoolgirl at her first dance, the birds sang their songs as though they were on the payroll of MGM, and in the distance a small dark figure would be seen winding its way up the path to the little cottage on the knoll that the old timers still called the little cottage on the knoll. —*Michele M. Ferrier*
San Francisco, California

In a matter of seconds Lillian had explained the passage of the seasons to the Reverend Hopwood, who was still blushing from her frank discussion of beans, which by no means had anyone confused. —*Charles Howland*
St. Paul, Minnesota

Mercilessly, like a sadistic nun, the rain beat down, drenching his brown—once gray until he touched it up—balding hair and running in meandering rivulets down his back between his Hanes Beefy-T and baby-smooth skin, all because he had carelessly forgotten his trusty fedora in the hallway on the antique washstand which his mother had given him and his wife refinished in a honey-pine stain for which she paid too much at the corner store since she was too lazy to take the short drive to the discount department store. —*Barbara J. Halladay*
Wolfe Island, Ontario

As the covered wagon rattled over the well-worn route, Katherine, who had never wanted to travel west, cursed her husband, cursed the wagon, cursed the heat of the day, and cursed the uncourteous people in the red Mazda

Miata who honked and gave her the finger as they went
zipping by.   —*K. H. McAlister*
                                              Calgary, Alberta

Mother Superior strode determinedly down the polished marble corridors of St. Isaac's, determined that today
was the day she was going, once and for all, to lay down the
law to Sister Maria, and proceeded, marching steadfastly
past flying-buttress rays of sunshine slanting through the
stained-glass windows until she reached the great oaken
double doors and flung them open, crying out, "Sister
Maria, I will no longer tolerate that filthy habit of yours!"
as Sister Maria, hearing the biting anger of Mother
Superior's voice, pushed her creeper out from underneath
the '57 Chevy Bel Air that she was lovingly restoring.

                                              —*Tom Butler*
                                              Tallahassee, Florida

While J.C. sat trembling with cold in the partially
enclosed bus shelter across the street from the capitol
building on this brutal winter day, he tried to remember
what had brought him from Dallas, Texas, to Madison,
Wisconsin, and then he remembered: it was a 1974
eggshell-blue Volkswagen Beetle.   —*J. C. Carver*
                                              Madison, Wisconsin

IT WAS A
DARK AND
STORMY
NIGHT

It was a dark and stormy night; the rain fell in torrents—except at occasional intervals, when it was checked by a violent gust of wind which swept up the streets (for it is in London that our scene lies), rattling along the housetops, and fiercely agitating the scanty flame of the lamps that struggled against the darkness.

"It was a dock and store, me knight, that burned down in the fire at the Royal Marina," the squire reported to Lancelot.
—*David K. Crandall*
Sherman Oaks, California

Watching the rain pour down, highlighted by the street lights outside his tenement window, Abe "Piano" Forte riffed through his vast collection of jazz LPs and thought contentedly, "It will be another Parker and Torme night."
—*Jim Ratzenberger*
Vienna, Virginia

It was a dark and stormy night in Chicago; the wind howled like a banshee, the windows rattled as if shaken by a drunken intruder, rains poured from the heavens by the celestial bucket full, thunder boomed like a cosmic wrecking ball suggesting apocalyptic visions of destruction;

unfortunately, all this was lost on Zelda, who had missed her connecting flight in Newark.

—*Caroline Kehne*
Clarenceville, Quebec

Her mood was dark, her name was Stormy, but, boy, what a nightie!

—*Paul Streeter*
Madbury, New Hampshire

"A thousand pardons, me lord, for returning without me noble master's supplies," pleaded the knight's squire as he fended off angry Sir Gawain's blows, "but the commissary's doors were bolted and I could see through a crack in the shutters that it was a darkened store, me knight."

—*Don O'Brien*
Indianapolis, Indiana

It was an occluded and fetid evening; the lights rolled in coruscating brisance down the Strip (for it is in Las Vegas that our story takes place) where Mel Torme, tormented by unwonted television satires, initiated a pattern of aberrant behavior that was to mar his career when he suddenly ripped all of his clothes and leaped, utterly naked, into the shocked and repulsed audience, and thus, for the first but not, alas, for the last time, it was a starkers Torme night.

—*Tom W. Gläser*
Hollywood, Florida

It was a starkly wormy rite, Pedro mused, as he stared at the caterpillar at the bottom of his tequila bottle, but he knew he had better swallow the vile corpse if the guys were to consider him macho.

—*Richard Heine*
Whittier, California

The night was restless after the Highlands victory, and obnoxious jubilation encircled the Round Table in its celebration feast, or nearly so, as that perfect geometry was interrupted by one knight's noticeable absence, and, although Arthur summoned him several times during the feast, the dark and stormy knight stayed responseless behind his locked chamber doors, brooding over the blank parchment at his fingertips, ink dry on his quill, the opening line to a novel relentlessly stuck in his head like an unyielding sword ground into anvil and stone.

—*John P. Doucet*
Raceland, Louisiana

Paul Clifford rested during his feverish search for the chickens that had disappeared so mysteriously during the high school graduation ceremonies, specifically dispatched to locate the hens that had been reported missing during the playing of Pomp and Circumstance, and, sitting in the loft pondering the significance of it all, was approached by an Englishman who, gazing at the crackling ovoid shape lying fractured beneath Clifford's trousers, asked him, "Have you hatched the lost eggs of pomp, eh?"

—*Larry Sherman*
Fremont, California

Mark looked out the window at the towering mountain and pondered his latest creation, a foundation garment with flexible stays, when suddenly the mountain erupted, totally covering all of his work, and it was to be 1500 years before the world would know of the elast stays of Pompeii.

—*Richard W. O'Bryan*
Perrysburg, Ohio

It was a dark and stormy July afternoon as the frenzied herd of fear-maddened bulls burst from the shambles of their flimsy enclosure, stampeding into the street (for it is in Pamplona that our scene lies), while overhead hovered swarms of angry mosquitoes, savoring, in their tiny insect minds, the delicious anticipation of that moment when the festival below would degenerate into a scene of chaos and carnage, if the headward bull were lit on!

—David Gordon Willingshofer
Vancouver, British Columbia

The zookeeper, Camels tucked in his shirt pocket, found himself caught equidistant between the unpredictable female elephant and the huge male, and he knew that his only chance was to retreat from her and bluff the male with the only thing the animal feared, namely, smoke, and so he mentally rehearsed his strategy, "Move bullward, light one."

—Richard Heine
Whittier, California

Sister May of the Passion seethed with anger (well, not really anger, since wrath is one of the seven deadly sins, but indignation surely); after all, she'd repeatedly warned the fourth-grade class that she would *not* tolerate any rude, disgusting noises or odors during the visits of important guests (even if the Ladies' Altar Society had been selling bean burritos at lunchtime to raise money for a new statue of the Infant of Prague, complete with guano-resistant crown) yet, just as the monsignor was about to bless the students, that vile, spoiled only child (whose parents probably practiced artificial contraception), that filthy heathen, little Eddie Bulwer, let one.

—Nancy Wambach
San Jose, California

He was an immense man, so huge, so intent, so ominous-looking yet so gentle that he would not contemplate even swatting a mosquito, but his principal fame was as a scientist and inventor, being renowned for the discovery of a new protective fabric called Lytin (a combination of Lycra, titanium, and nylon), which was so impentrable that it was widely used in bullet-proof vests, but that is another story; meantime, a prime example of the vast contradiction of appearance and reality is the story that, during the screening of *The Sun Also Rises*, he was moved to tears during the bullfight scene, and was overheard to say, "Oh, it would still be alive today if only the bull wore Lytin.

—*Fred Mason*
Dunwoody, Georgia

It was a Victorian Christmas and everyone was there—that little dickens, Charlie, Anthony and his trollope, and hardy old Thomas; the butler Samuel was trying to make-peace between Thackeray and wilde young man Oscar; H. Rider was looking haggard and each person there was feeling yonge and acting like a newman, groups gathered about listening to Lewis carroll and Charles reade from his latest works; and they cried out for moore in the gissing-game where Henry and James (the Bostonian ambassadors) were imitating a brontesaurus (to borrow a page from Darwin's *Eliot and the Odyssey*)—but, to the disappointment of all, the sentence ended without the obligatory pun on the name Bulwer-Lytton.

—*Dave DalSasso*
Bethlehem, Pennsylvania